and books

ANCIENT EGYPT - A Survey

Elfriede Preger

and books

around publishing/the distributors

south bend, indiana

Library of Congress Catalog Number
78-54099

International Standard Book Number
ISBN 0-89708-001-7

and books are published by
around publishing/the distributors

Manufactured in the United States of America
Hardesty Printing, Rochester, Indiana
Third Printing, 1978

Additional copies available:

        and books
        the distributors
        702 South Michigan
        South Bend, IN 46618 U.S.A.

TABLE OF CONTENTS

COVER

WEIGHING OF THE HEART OF THE SCRIBE ANI

A papyrus of approx. 1250 B.C. from the "Book of the Dead" of Ani, sacerdotal scribe to Nefer-ta-ri ("Beautiful Companion"), favourite wife of Ramesses II, in her funerary temple. Ani wrote a Book of Instructions, called "The Maxims of Ani."

The "Judgment of the dead king" had already existed as part of the "Pyramid Texts" of Dynasties V and VI. The king, in order to gain admission to the solar bark, must be pure, just, and perfect. A "passer" transporting souls over the lake at the entrance to the afterworld put questions to the the king regarding his justice, purity, and integrity. The king could not pass unless all answers were given satisfactorily.

With the gaining of prominence of the Osirian faith, this idea extended to all men; they would be judged and have to answer before the tribunal. Slowly the belief crystallised into the "Tribunal of the Dead" with Osiris as the judge and the nome (district) gods as assessors; the latter numbered forty-two in accordance with the final number of districts into which the country was divided.

Thoth, god of the scribes and scribe of the gods, acted as secretary to the court, with Horus and Anubis as co-adjutants making sure that the scales in the weighing of the heart were correct.

Ani, in order to achieve survival in the after-life and to be identified with Osiris, is here tested and declared "true of voice" in the Hall of Judgment. Coming into the presence of the assessor gods in the upper register, followed by his wife Tutu who holds a sistrum with a Hathor-headed handle identifying her as a priestess of the goddess, Ani proceeds towards the scale.

In its pans are placed the heart of Ani, the feather of Ma'at, goddess of Truth, respectively. The heart in Egyptian belief was the seat of intelligence. The weight of the heart is not to exceed that of the feather, lest it will be eaten by the hybrid monster Ammut, "Devourer of hearts," part lioness, hippopotamus, and crocodile, waiting behind Thoth, with his palette and reed brush. The baboon above the upright of the scale is also an incarnation animal of the god of writing; the figure atop a brick represents the "brick on which the deceased's mother gave birth" to Ani. The human-headed bird represents BA, the soul, while the female standing figures in front of Ani are symbolic of the fates (SHAY) of the dead.

The proceedings begin with Ani addressing each of the assessor gods by name to show that he knows and does not fear them, making a "negative confession" to each of them, of forty-two specified sins related to behaviour in life and indicative of the general moral attitude of ancient Egypt.

After being declared "true (or right) of voice" = Ma'at-kherou, Ani is led into the presence of Osiris.

In accordance with artistic canons, the flesh tone for Ani is rendered darker than that for his wife.

FOREWORD

by Dr. William G. Dever, *Director*
W. F. Albright Institute of Archaeological Research in Jerusalem

I am happy to write a foreword to the excellent outline of ancient Egyptian culture which Mrs. Preger has produced. I can claim no direct contribution to the present volume except that I encouraged Mrs. Preger to undertake it, and I gladly yielded to her any rights of publication I had. That she has carried the project to completion, largely with her own resources, is to her credit.

The result is a succinct handbook of ancient Egyptian history and culture. It is based on reliable authorities but is written in non-technical language. It is arranged topically for easy reference and is well illustrated by carefully chosen objects, including many from the Herbert Edgar Clark Collection at the Y.M.C.A. in Jerusalem. I recommend this book without hesitation to the general reader who, like so many of us, has become fascinated by Egyptology. The student will find it a valuable resume, and even the specialist can consult it with profit. I hope that this book will find a wide and responsive audience, and that it will serve to focus attention on a superb collection that deserves to be more widely known.

It is by far beyond the limitations of this compilation to include even one example of all the many facets of the arts and crafts, sciences and so on, from ancient Egypt. Whatever is offered will hopefully create enough interest in the reader to have a closer look at this immensely interesting and wide-ranging part of man's history.

—E.P.

ACKNOWLEDGEMENTS

I wish to thank the following persons who were of help in my efforts to compile this handbook:

Dr. William G. Dever, Director of the W. F. Albright Institute or Archeology, Jerusalem, for granting me (professional) permission to carry out the work at the Clark Collection.

The Rev. Father Couroyer, Egyptologist, for his kind help in identifying some of the scarabs from the collection.

Ms. Helen Myer, for many years part-time administrator of the collection, who, despite her recent retirement, volunteered her services by giving me access to documents, making contact with a number of authorities in the field, etc.

My work on the collection was made enjoyable by the ready cooperation of Mr. Clarence Schmidt, General Director of the Y.M.C.A., Jerusalem, and the friendliness and helpfulness of his staff.

I am greatly indebted to Dr. Marian Feigenbaum, San Francisco, who in such a tactful manner weeded out many oddities of my written English, her editorial pen hopefully having caught all of them.

To Phyllis Bosley goes my gratitude for much help.

Without the genial and patient guidance of Vernon L. Gregory, San Francisco, I would have never grasped the most elementary aspects of the technical arrangement of this catalogue.

Last but not least I thank my husband whose patience and faith in my "compiler's talents" left me free to relegate the more mundane aspects of my duties to a less time-consuming level than usual.

OUTLINE OF POLITICAL AND CULTURAL HISTORY

Traces of human habitation in the Nile Valley from before the Prehistoric Period are described by the terms used for European Prehistory: Palaeolithic, Mesolithic, Neolithic. In the Nile Valley and the bordering desert lands the Prehistoric Period is represented by roughly shaped flint tools of large size, and smaller scrapers. They appear to have been produced during Palaeolithic times, and were of a type used throughout the Ancient Near East.

Since all of North Africa was, throughout the Palaeolithic Period, inhabited, the hunter and nomad population left its traces uniformly over the area. When drastic climatic changes at the end of this era, caused by retreat of the ice-cap in Europe, transformed pastures into desert, man's habitat moved into the Nile region. It is from that time that domestic refuse heaps attest to a settled occupation of man. The use of flint developed into the production of much finer, smaller tools for particular uses including arrowheads and serrated blades, referred to as sickle blades. The latter possibly indicates the growing of cereal, although no direct evidence for this assumption as yet exists. Evidence for this is positively provided only during the Neolithic Period from which sites were discovered on the western edge of the Delta, the Fayum and Middle Egypt.

From these sites comes irrefutable proof of settled agricultural life. Crops and cereals were cultivated, linen and baskets produced, also crude pottery and a great variety of stone and flint tools.

The early settlers inhabited a valley of reed swamps and shallows formed by the annual Nile floods, teeming with hippopotami, crocodiles, fish and fowl. The wadis alongside the river supported, with their shrubs and meadows, lions, wild cattle, ass, ibex, antelope and other desert game, all of which were represented in Egyptian art throughout prehistoric and historic times.

To the unlettered cultures immediately preceding Egypt's Dynastic Period the terms Early and Late Predynastic are usually applied. Many cultures from the period are also named after the sites where remains were first found. Site names for these cultures should not, however, be used in too close association with the respective sites, but rather the less confusing terms Early or Late Predynastic.

The Early Predynastic Period commenced at the end of the Neolithic and continued into the Chalcolithic Period, roughly covering the time from 5000 B.C. to 3600 B.C. The main cultures during this period, situated in Lower, i.e. Northern Egypt, were:

1) Fayum "A" 2) Merimda

and in Upper, i.e. Southern Egypt:

1) Deir Tasa 2) el-Badari 3) el-Amra

The Tasian culture, remains of which were also found in Middle Egypt, is considered by some authorities to be a phase of the Badarian culture.

From the Badarian culture come the earliest copper objects found in Egypt. The use of this metal was not as yet common; the production of copper tools and weapons was a gradual process. Pearshaped heads of metal attached to maces became common during the Amartian, i.e. late Early Predynastic Period. The throw-stick for fowling was used from at least early predynastic times on. The continuation of its use into late Pharaonic times is attested to by many tomb paintings, etc.

The idea of after-life clearly existed in Egypt at this early date. The dead were buried away from the village of Deir Tasa, while in earlier times burials took place in or near the house of the deceased. In the Badarian Period the body, in flexed position, was placed into a shallow grave, the hot dry sand acting as a desiccating agent. Often the dead were wrapped in animal skins or basketwork; they were provided with a great variety of objects to supply the needs of after-life. (I).

In pottery, the Badarian Period saw the development of a particularly fine, usually remarkably thin ware of many different shapes, provided with a red polish and a blackened top. This ware was to become common during much later periods. For the first time the human figure was modelled. Funerary offerings in the form of terracotta, ivory or bone figures of females, their procreative attributes emphasized, come from this culture. Chronologically and in iconography they strongly resemble figures from another part of the Near East. Stone vases were first manufactured in the Badarian period. The use of flint, ivory and bone was perfected and from that time dates the first glazing of steatite beads.

An important find from Badarian times, where they were common, are the slate palettes for grinding malachite.

Copper jewellery such as small bars, beads and pins, and later weapons and tools of copper were known through vigorous trade contacts with Asia. However, tools for the grinding of stone vessels, carving of ivory and reaping of grain continued to be made of flint.

The Late Predynastic Period from approx. 3600–3200 B. C. is usually divided into Nakada I and Nakada II, from the cemetery site in Upper Egypt. The discovery of the Nakada cemetery was made by Sir Flinders Petrie in 1894. He devised a sequence dating for prehistoric objects from Egypt which is still in use.

Knowledge based on material evidence of Nakada I is very scanty. The culture of Nakada II has also been identified at el-Girza, north of Maidum in the Fayum; the period is, therefore, usually referred to as Gerzean. In Lower Egypt the main site from this period is el-Maadi.

While the highly polished dark red ware with carbonized rims from the Badarian Period remained in general use, pottery of the Gerzean culture is distinguished by a number of characteristic shapes and designs. Wavy-handled jars of light pink or buff ware, decorated with primitive shrines, boats, human figures, animals, plants are a hallmark of the period. Some of the pots simulate in shape the stone vases which by now were common due to the introduction of the cranked flint borer.

Burials at el-Maadi were more elaborate than those in Upper Egypt. Graves were more carefully constructed with wood and matting revetting, sometimes of more than one compartment. More superior funerary offerings were placed in the graves of Lower Egypt than in those of contemporary Upper Egypt. The inference taken from these factors is that a higher standard of culture was maintained in Lower Egypt than in Upper Egypt.

Slate palettes, already known from Badarian graves, are now found generally, many in animal form. They are the most common objects from the Predynastic Period.

Nothing is clearly known about political organizations in Lower and Upper Egypt during early predynastic times. Two loose confederations seem to have existed, made up of communities which may have corresponded to the later nomes. Increased political activity, however, becomes evident in the late Gerzean Period, i.e. approx. 3400–3200 B. C. with the two confederations more clearly defined. The "king" of Lower Egypt now wears the red crown as distinct from the white one of Upper Egypt. These crowns were to remain royal insigniae for the kings of "the two lands" throughout Egypt's history. The existence of two capital cities, Buto in the Delta and Hierankopolis in Upper Egypt, furthermore indicates political turmoil as represented in a number of votive objects, mainly palettes and maceheads. The most important of these, historically, is the palette of King Menes or Nar-mer wearing the red and white crown on the respective sides of the object. He united the two regions and became the founder of Dynasty I.

Egypt was divided into the two principal regions from earliest times. Upper Egypt, called, during the dynastic period, Shemau, comprised twenty-two nomes, the Greek term for administrative districts. The first of these was Elephantine (modern Aswan), and the twenty-second Aphroditopolis (modern Atfih), south of Cairo. The Fayum was the twenty-first nome. Lower Egypt, the To-mehu ("Northern Land") of ancient times, consisting chiefly of the Delta, was then a largely undeveloped marsh and shrub area. Its division into nomes, consequently, experienced sporadic modification as development took place. The ultimate number of nomes was twenty, with Memphis the first. The nomes were, throughout the historic period, economical and fiscal units, even though boundaries, official names etc. changed in keeping with political and social changes that occurred. The worship of local gods, and taboos of the individual nomes were faithfully observed, notwithstanding locality changes within a nome. The eventual total of forty-one nomes for Egypt equalled the number of judges assisting Osiris in his tribunal of the soul of the deceased.

Basically, Egypt was and is the part of the Nile Valley that is cultivated. The cultivated area in antiquity was determined by the height to which the Nile rose during its annual inundation. June 15th was the date empirically fixed as the beginning of the year in ancient Egypt, since the Nile began to rise at approximately that time. The increase of the flood took place during August, and reached its height in September, remaining stationary for about three weeks, with a further slight rise in October, then falling gradually until the lowest level was reached in May.

Stationed along the Nile Valley were Nilometers recording the levels to which the river rose, as too high or too low waters were equally disastrous for the farming of the land. The river itself was called Iteru and the spirit of the Nile, a deity represented as the god of the Nile inundation, a man with full, pendulous breasts and a clump of papyrus on his head, Hapy. The flood was thus called the "arrival of Hapy." Aside from the watering of the fields by the flooding, the Nile brought with it a deposit of rich alluvium which acted as a regular fertilising agent. This black deposit gave the name KEME ("The Black") to the originally inhabited, cultivated land, while the uninhabited tawny-coloured desert was called DESHRET ("The Red").

The first truly historic period of Egypt begins with the unification of "the two lands" and the development of writing from its rudimentary form, as seen on some predynastic antiquities, into hieroglyphics. The period derives its name from the thirty-one dynasties into which Egypt was divided according to a scheme by the Ptolemaic priest-historian Manetho. Egyptologists later divided the Dynastic Period, lasting from approx. 3200–332 B. C., into shorter, distinct periods:

EARLY DYNASTIC (Dyn. I and II), also called Thinite or Archaic Period, approx. 3200-2686 B. C. After the unification of the country, important administrative reorganizations occurred, and the capital was established at Memphis, situated at the junction of Lower and Upper Egypt. Traditionally, Menes or Nar-mer, founder of Dynasty I, is credited with the foundation of Het-ka-ptah, one of the ancient names of Memphis, translating into "House of Ptah" which later became the derivative for the Greek Aigyptos, hence Egypt. The tombs from this period are at Sakkara and cenotaphs at Abydos. The earliest architectural elements of stone in Egypt were found in these tombs. Lapis lazuli and ebony objects, among others, indicate already existing trade connections with Asia and tropical Africa. Not enough material remains from this period have been found to shed light on political events, however.

During Dynasty II, funerary bas-reliefs and sculpture were produced, as well as vessels of alabaster, basalt, and diorite of outstanding excellence. Evidence of the sati-burial begins to disappear. Private burials near the tomb or cenotaph of the king became the custom. Gradually, stone replaced brick for building.

OLD KINGDOM (Dyn. III-VI), 2686–2181 B. C.: The capital was at Memphis, and the royal necropoloi at Giza and Sakkara. During the reign of King Neter-khet or Djoser of Dynasty III large-scale building and sculpture in stone was carried out. His step-pyramid at Sakkara was the creation of the first artist-architect known by name, Imhotep.

By the end of the Archaic Period, writing had advanced to a degree that the hieroglyphics had become an effective vehicle for use in continuous narration. This advance plus the improvement in the technique of arts and crafts ushered in a new artistic sophistication that was a strong contrast to the stiffness of the archaic culture of the preceding period. Private mastabas for nobles, no longer built only in brick but also stone, were erected near the royal tombs.

Dynasty IV, lasting from approx. 2613–2494 B. C., is called the Classic Age of the Old Kingdom. It was during this time that the true pyramid was evolved and reached its climax of development. The three great pyramids at Giza were all built within a span of seventy years by the kings Khufu or Cheops, Khafre or Chefren and Menkaure or Mycerinus. Local limestone was used for the interior and the highly prized type from Tura for the outer casing. Generally, a great mastery of the craftsman over most materials was achieved during this era.

No pyramids on the scale of those from Dynasty IV were ever again attempted; the kings of Dynasties V and VI had theirs erected at Abusir and Sakkara on a much humbler scale. Concurrently with the decrease in stature of the king during this time (previously identified with god, he now became the son of god) an increased influence of the sun-god Re at Heliopolis with its cult centering around the ben-ben or obelisk, developed.

Private mastabas gradually became larger, and rock-tombs were built for the nomarchs of provincial centres, indicating the assumption of power by the district governors over royal authority. Coupled with the rise of feudalism, the decentralization of government led to anarchy and strife among local princes, ending in political collapse. The first references of expeditions to the "Land of Punt," which were to continue throughout the historic period of Egypt, are from Dynasty V. An important feature of tombs from this time were the Pyramid Texts. Walls of the vestibule and burial chamber were covered with religious texts referring to the king's fate in after-life. They continued to be made during Dynasty VI. Sculpture for private persons, both in stone and particularly wood, attained a degree of highest excellence, to show signs of decadence during the next dynasty. With the ninety-four year reign of King Phiops II or Pepy II coming to an end, so does the Old Kingdom. A papyrus from the time vividly describes conditions at that ruinous stage of Egypt's history.

During the FIRST INTERMEDIATE PERIOD (Dyn. VII-X), 2181–2050 B. C., social and political strife, and struggle for power between leaders of the various localities, marked the day. Egypt was divided into many political entities. A succession of strong men tried in vain to restore the old peace and order. A strong and unchecked influx of foreigners in search of rich pastures took place, unhindered because of the internal turmoil of the country. All the arts of the period show a decline, an unsuccessful attempt to model themselves on Memphite prototypes. Dynasties IX and X were formed by a powerful ruling family from Heracleopolis in Upper Egypt who consolidated their power to expel the Asiatics from the Delta, and fortified the eastern borders. Eventually, their war against the princes at Thebes was won by the latter and the country was re-unified under one king.

MIDDLE KINGDOM (Dyn. XI and XII), 2050–1786 B. C. The capital of the country was now at Thebes. Under the fifty-one year reign of the first king, Menthu-hotep I Neb-hepet--re, Egypt was pacified and partly regained her former prosperity. This king was still worshipped as a local hero some one thousand years after his death. Campaigns against Libyans and Nubians followed the re-establishment of a centralized administration. For the royal burial a large rock-tomb with a pyramid in the forecourt, based on a highly original plan, was erected at Deir-el Bahri. Royal coffins, fitted with a flat lid, were made of stone. Commonly used were inner and outer coffins of wood of a chest type. The most important part of their decoration were the "Coffin Texts," excerpts from funerary texts and derived from the Pyramid Texts of Dynasties V and VI. A refined style of drawing and carving is shown in the reliefs from the last years of this reign.

The two succeeding kings of Dynasty XI inherited a country tranquil and united. Dynasty XII, with royal residences first at Thebes, and, later at Dashur, Lisht, Lahun and Hawara (Fayum) showed a particularly strong activity in foreign affairs. All its kings followed a pattern set by the first, Amun-em-het I = "Amun-is-first," or Ammenemes I who, as vizier to the last ruler of Dynasty XI apparently came to the throne on either the former's death or a breakdown of government. The very powerful Dynasty XII created a highly organized, well administered Egypt. Nubia was annexed to the country, and a fortification called the "Wall of the Prince" constructed to keep out the continuous waves of infiltrating Asiatics.

Egypt was in contact with Palestine and Syria as witnessed by respective finds in these countries. "The Story of Sinuhe" bears testimony to regular journeys to Syria by envoys of the Egyptian kings. Expeditions by sea were once more sent to Punt and regular trade was instituted with Crete.

From the beginning of Dynasty XII, it became the rule for the king to have as his intended successor his eldest son acting as co-regent, to ensure continuity of a strong government. The political disintegration at the end of the Old Kingdom having been principally a result of the independence and increased power of the nomarchs, the kings of the early Dynasty XII severely curbed these powers. Under the reign of Sen-wosret III or Sesostris III the office of nomarch was apparently abolished altogether; from 1860 B. C. onwards there is no longer any mentioning of nomarchs and no tombs for them were built in the respective province-cemeteries.

Dynasty XII was at the height of its power under Sesostris III who reigned from 1878–1843 B. C. The southern frontier of Egypt in this period was established south of the second cataract at Semna. From there to Elephantine (Aswan) a series of protective fortresses were erected. In the latter area Sesostris III, having been deified in the New Kingdom, was worshipped. Portraits of him show a man of forceful determination, stern, and with a great deal of weariness. Portraiture of the time is said to be of brutal realism. It does, in fact, display, for the first time in royal likenesses, an expression of human qualities and a never-again-equalled degree of vigour. This is in strong contrast to the earlier idealized portraits of kings, intended to convey a god-like, youthful image. The arts generally were at an exceptionally high level of perfection. Jewellery from Dynasty XII was, on the whole, of a much more refined and superbly executed type than that of the New Kingdom. The "Pessimistic Literature" of the Middle Kingdom reflects the chaotic conditions its rulers had inherited. The phase of the language from the time, considered by the Egyptians themselves as the classic, is given the name "Middle Egyptian." It was to be the model for literary compositions until Roman times. As in the royal sculpture of Dynasty XII, the literature of the Middle Kingdom has a haunting power of its own. Like the former, it conveys the idea of the king not as god, but rather superman.

Pyramids of the rulers of Dynasty XII were built of stone rubble along the desert margins of the Fayum. The last king of importance of Dynasty XII, Amen-em-het III greatly improved conditions in the Fayum by large irrigation schemes etc. The so-called labyrinth, a hugh funerary structure he had built there, was famous in classical times and still stood in the fifth century B. C. to be recorded by Herodotus. Re-building of many sites was undertaken during the nearly fifty-year reign of that king. After Amen-em-het III's death, his by then already aged son reigned for eight years, continuing a dynasty which had begun to pass into decline, and was followed on the throne by his sister. In 1786 B. C. the XIIth Dynasty and with it the Middle Kingdom broke down.

The SECOND INTERMEDIATE PERIOD is the time between Dynasties XIII and XVIII, lasting from 1767-1565 B. C. It comprised three native and two Hyksos dynasties, the latter distinguished as the Great and the Lesser Hyksos. The historical sequence of the time has not been clearly established; overlapping between dynasties seems to have taken place.

The decadence of state organization which began to develop from Dynasty XIII on gave the Asiatic settlers in the Delta the opportunity to establish a separate kingdom with the capital at Tanis (Avaris) and with Seth as the god of their worship, modelled perhaps on Baal. These foreign settlements, probably comprising Semites and Hurrians, were a product of the periodic chaotic conditions, from the First Intermediate Period onwards, which allowed unchecked immigration of foreigners.

The Great Hyksos of Dynasty XV, begun approx. 1670 B. C., later extended their power over all of Egypt but did not rule in Thebes where, eventually, the war of liberation against them, ending with their expulsion from Egypt, took place. The Hyksos = hekau-khasut, i.e. "Princes of foreign countries" maintained artistic traditions of Egypt and enthusiastically adopted many artistic ideas and customs. During their rule, scarabs were produced in enormous numbers. Many of them, bearing Hyksos names, were found in Palestine and the Sudan. These and other antiquities found in Crete and West Asia testify to expanded foreign contacts during Hyksos rule. Their kings took native names and fostered local culture in many ways. During Dynasty XIX and later a tradition, related by Manetho, of the Hyksos as cruel and merciless rulers over the native population was publicized. Material evidence, however, indicates the propagandistic inaccuracy of this theory. In fact, the Hyksos rule was one of the greatly fertilizing influences in Egyptian civilization. During this time bronze came into general use in Egypt. A completely new range of weapons, the horse-drawn chariot and scale-armour were introduced, to be used in the conflicts between the Hyksos and the Theban princes. The Blue or Battle Crown which kings of Dynasty XVIII and later are often shown wearing, was added to the ruler's regalia during the Hyksos era. It was a leather helmet to which gilded metal disks were sewn. The vertical loom was an innovation of the Hyksos in Egypt. The long-necked flute, round or rectangular tambourine, lyre and oboe of Egyptian music-making were of Hyksos origin in that country. They also imported into Egypt the olive tree and pomegranate.

Dynasty XVII, begun approx. 1650 B. C. consisted of two groups of Theban rulers, one of whom acknowledged the suzerainty of the Hyksos, while the other asserted their right to the kingship over all of Egypt. The ensuing clashes of the latter group of Theban princes with the Hyksos, culminating in the battle before the capital of Avaris itself, brought about the end of the period.

The NEW KINGDOM, approx. 1567–1085 B. C., includes Dynasties XVIII and XIX as well as the continuing Ramesside Period of Dynasty XX. It represents the last of the periods of greatness in Egypt. Dynasty XVIII is characterized by what is called the first internationalism. Egypt achieved the maximum expanse of her imperial and commercial power during the New Kingdom. Nubia and Kush were under the rule of Egyptian viceroys, new dependencies in Palestine and Syria were brought into life, diplomatic relations with the Aegean, Cyprus, Anatolia and Babylon were established. Towards the end of Dynasty XVIII, Egypt lost some of her influence in Asia, concurrent with the rise of the Hittites. During Dynasty XIX, Egypt attempted to challenge this new threat but finally had to enter into a treaty with the Hittites.

The revival of the reunited country was marked by temple building, particularly at Karnak. Several generations worked on the building of the gigantic national temple to Amun-Re. Karnak translates into "Counter of the Places." The Egyptian word is ipet-iset, meaning the assembly-place of all the Egyptian deities who had their own chapels in the national temple, where they were worshipped as "visiting gods."

A renaissance of art took place, taking its inspiration from the best of the Middle Kingdom. Tuthmosis I, reigning from 1525–1512 B. C., was the first king to have his tomb built on the west bank of the Nile at Thebes, in the Valley of the Kings. Throughout the New Kingdom, this remained the royal burial place. In tombs of wealthy persons, from the New Kingdom onwards, a "Book of the Dead," written on papyrus or leather, was placed. Included in it, among other texts, were incantations encompassing all aspects of Egyptian religion, entitled "Formulae for going forth by day," read out at the funerary ceremony by the priest. Coloured vignettes with fine line drawings accompanied the texts of these books.

The New Kingdom and especially Dynasty XVIII are, from the point of material remains of often great intrinsic value, the best-known eras of Egyptian history. Politically, the most important kings of Dynasty XVIII were, after the founder, Ahmosis, Tuthmosis I, Hatshepsut, Tuthmosis III. Queen Hatshepsut had usurped the throne from her half-brother and stepson after first acting as regent for him. She ruled over all of Egypt with complete control for some twenty years, sent an important trading expedition to Punt, and ushered in a period of domestic development in which peaceful trade and artistic activities were the main features. On her death, Tuthmosis III regained the throne, carrying out a vigorous martial policy including a victorious battle against rebellious subject princes at Megiddo in Palestine.

On Amenophis III's accession to the throne in 1417 B. C., the fortunes of Egypt had reached their zenith. With secure borders, good foreign relations and settled conditions at home he could divert his attention to the building of temples, erecting obelisks and, in general, fostering the arts. The "Colossus of Memnon" and its companion piece were statues of Amenophis III and originally stood at the entrance to the temple, each carved from a single block of sandstone. Evidence indicates that the realistic tendencies in art generally associated with the Amarna period of his son and successor had actually been established during the reign of Tuthmosis III. The same applies to the cult of the sun-disk, confirmed by a scarab and a stela among other objects. The reign of Amenophis IV was marked by his open rebellion against the now extremely powerful and influential priesthood of Amun-Re and by the attempt to have the sun-disk Aten worshipped as the sole god of the formerly polytheistic religion. He moved his capital from Thebes to a newly constructed site in Middle Egypt, Akhetaten or "Horizon-of-the-Aten," the modern Tell el-Amarna. The worship of all other gods was henceforth proscribed. Monotheism did not, however, outlive Akhenaten ("Serviceable-to-Aten," as he renamed himself) long, partly because he took no interest in preserving the magnificent empire he had inherited and so opened the way to a gradual decrease in the fortunes of Egyptian foreign policies, etc. His own unusual physique, attributed to a possible endocrine deficiency, apparently dictated the revolutionary portrait style of a crudely veristic nature bordering very often on caricature. This extended beyond royal portraiture to create likenesses in the "Amarna style" in general.

The very brief reign of Akhenaten's half-brother was followed by that of the boy-king Tut-ankh-aten. After he had been on the throne for a few years, the priesthood of Amun-Re regained its power. The old religious order restored, the king changed his name to Tut-ankh-amun = "All-life-is-in-Amun" and moved back to the old capital of Thebes. During the massive grave robbing that occurred in the Ramesside era, Tut-ankh-amun's was the only one left more or less intact because his royal status was not great enough to consider the possible contents of his tomb too highly. His tomb, in fact, yielded a great number of funerary objects of all descriptions, including elaborate jewellery, which made an otherwise obscure king into the most well-known of Egypt. The opulence of some of the items from his tomb gives an idea as to what priceless treasures the tombs of his more important predecessors and successors must have contained.

The "Amarna Letters," written in Akkadian, the lingua franca of the time, in cuneiform script, are the diplomatic correspondence of the period. In it, Tut-ankh-amun's widow figures as the only Egyptian queen of whom any personal correspondence was found. She asks the king of the Hittites "to send me one of your sons, and he shall be ruler of Egypt and my husband." After Tut-ankh-amun, an elderly noble ruled for a short period and was succeeded by a non-royal person who had been chief adviser to both Akhenaten and Tut-ankh-amun, his reign serving a transitory role between Dynasties XVIII and XIX.

The family of Ramesses came from the Delta. The first of its members to become king was formerly vizier to Horemhab, last ruler of Dynasty XVII. Later in the period the capital was moved to Piramese in the Delta, on the site of the old Hyksos stronghold Avaris.

Rameses II stands out as a ruler for sixty-seven years, with six Great Wives and over a hundred "royal children" all of whose names were commemorated in stone carving. His reputation as the king par excellence rests largely on the erection of colossal statues of himself throughout Egypt, many usurped from predecessors and his name substituted for theirs in the cartouches; as well as the celebration of his unquestionable political ability and military victories in some of the longest texts in Egyptian literature. Temples on a gigantic scale were built and additions to existing buildings carried out. He completed the temple at Abydos to Osiris with the famous king-list of seventy-eight of his predecessors. The most remarkable monument to himself was the Nubian rock-temple at Abu Simbel with four colossal figures of the king. His own artistic style was to be followed by the whole period. It seems that the Exodus of the Khabiru, regarded by some scholars as the Hebrews, took place during his reign, or that of his successor. Under the last great king of the New Kingdom, Ramesses III of Dynasty XX, the mass onslaught of the Meshwesh from Libya was largely repelled. Parties of them, nevertheless, took service in the Egyptian armies to form, gradually, an influential military caste. The attacks of the Libyans took place in coalition with a variety of the Sea Peoples including the Philistines. Many incidents from these battles are immortalized on the walls of Medinet Habu, a sanctuary at the southern part of West Thebes with funerary temples including that of Ramesses III. The first great sea battle of which details are recorded was that between the invading fleet of the Philistines and the Egyptians at one of the mouths of the Nile in which the attackers were largely destroyed.

Dynasty XX is distinguished in Egypt's history by the revival of her glory and prosperity as well as by attacks from outside which heralded the impending loss of her imperial strength. From the death of Ramesses III in 1166 B. C., possibly by a harim assassination, until the end of the Dynasty and the New Kingdom, in 1085 B. C., eight more kings of the same name reigned. In this period falls the wholesale pillaging of royal tombs, often with official connivance, including the violation of the mummies. Many documents of investigation and legal actions in connection with these thefts are preserved. Egypt lost the remaining part of her Asiatic empire, resulting in serious economic consequences. Hieratic, a cursive script adapted from the hieroglyphics for speedier writing, had been in use for documents of secular nature from Dynasty V onwards. It remained in regular use until the end of the New Kingdom for administrative purposes, legal and official documents, and educational and scientific literature, particularly on papyrus. This material remained the most important used for writing throughout ancient Egyptian history. The Greek word papuros was used from the fourth or third century B. C. on. Its origin is unknown but as Papouro translates into "that of a king" and in Greek times the production of papyrus was a royal monopoly, it may refer to this latter fact.

Egypt's power was divided at the end of Dynasty XX between the High Priest of Amun-Re at Thebes and the Vizier of Lower Egypt. This state of affairs continued into the *LATE DYNASTIC PERIOD, the whole of which lasted from 1085–332 B. C.* At Tanis in the Delta reigned kings of Dynasty XXI, while simultaneously at Thebes, the dynasty of the High Priests ruled until 935 B. C. The latter attempted the establishment of a religious regime in peaceful coexistence with the secular ruler at Tanis. They carried out the salvage of the royal tombs not touched by the scandalous plunderings during Dynasty XX and those mummies that had been damaged were re-wrapped and re-buried at a hiding place in a cache at Deir el-Bahri in the Valley of the Kings, where they remained until the late nineteenth century A. D.

From approx. 1000 B. C. on, as a title suggesting a person of splendour and great antiquity, the king was called Pharaoh. (Egyptian Per-o, meaning "Great House"). It was never, however, the full and proper title of the king which in the official version consisted of five names.

After the tenth century B. C., iron was in general use in Egypt for tools and weapons. Very few royal burials have been discovered of a date later than the end of the New Kingdom, indicating that political changes of fortune affected the evolution of funerary architecture, and, together with the scarcity of suitable burial lands near the principal sites, necessitated the fitting of tombs among earlier ones.

In 935 B. C., one of the Libyan families that had settled as mercenaries in Egypt centuries before came to power and, favoured by the king at Tanis, succeeded him as Dynasty XXII with the capital at Bubastis. Unlike other African ethnic groups, the Meshwesh and Libu of Libya had blue eyes and blond hair. The first king, Sheshonq I, in one of his campaigns against Palestine, pillaged the treasures of the temple in Jerusalem. To judge by the scanty records from the time, Egypt was soon in a very unsettled state, with a parallel line of rulers to the Libyans in power. A disintegration of the state into smaller states, based on activities of subversive groups in different parts of the country due to the lack of a strong central government, took place and came to a head in mid-eight century B. C. Aside from it, the Mass, meaning "Lord" and a term still used in the context in Tuareg-Berber speech, of the Meshwesh and those of the Libu, had created separate principalities. This feudal anarchy resulted in there being two ruling dynasties in about 800 B. C. and four by 750 B. C. An embroidered account recalls this political situation, retold as part of the war-legends of one of the contemporary pharaohs.

The Pyramid Texts of the Old Kingdom were studied and used in private burials. Little monumental art was created during the Libyan Period but beautiful bronzes and jewellery produced. The latter was often worked either of silver or electrum, ("green gold") inlaid with glass or glass paste, or with semiprecious stones, or of bronze fitted with a layer of gold to give life and colour to the former metal. The famous "Egyptian blue" (a crystalline lapis lazuli material artifically produced since Dynasty IV to replace the expensive imported lapis lazuli from Afghanistan) was extensively utilized in jewellery. This coeruleum of Pliny's description, was so sought after that it became an export article to the Roman Empire as the standard blue pigment for wall-painting. It continued in use until the seventh century A. D. Increased use of the harder stones such as schist and basalt was made during the Libyan Period for sculpture, and continued to be favoured after that.

One of the common features in Egyptian portraiture, that of elongating eyes and eyebrows beyond the cheekbones, disappeared after the New Kingdom.

In approx. 751 B. C., a native king from Napata near the fourth cataract in the Sudan (called Kush by the Egyptians), whose people had preserved many Egyptian customs, including the worship of Amun-Re captured the throne of Egypt in the name of order and of orthodoxy of religion. This Kushite or Ethiopian Dynasty XXV established its rule with relative ease because of the prevailing disunity in the land. Its capitals were at Thebes and Tanis, and its kings expressed devotion to Amun-Re by investing significant powers at Thebes to the Divine Adoratrix, usually a royal princess acting as priestess. The king and ruling class in general were so imbued with native Egyptian culture that they began the renaissance of the arts which was to reach its climax in the next reign. The artistic activity and achievement of the period was unrivalled since the early part of Ramesside times. The celebrated realism of portraiture in depicting age, attributed to Saite artists is, in fact, a feature of the Kushite Dynasty.

Dynasty XXVI, also known as the Saite Period, was one of renewed order and prosperity for the country under native rulers from Sais, and lasted for more than a century. Royal residences were at Memphis and Sais, but the latter was mainly used as the burial place of the kings. Major sites from the period were Edfu, Sakkara, Daphnae, and Naucratis. The revival of cultural and artistic life begun under Dynasty XXV attained spendid proportions during this period, from 664–525 B. C. An intensive study of antiquities from the past characterizes all arts and crafts from that time. Temples were restored, and additions carried out. Sculpture in particular was modelled on Old Kingdom and Middle Kingdom examples, extending even to the dress of former periods. This style is often referred to as Neo-Memphite art. Saite sculpture shows a very high degree of surface work. A characteristic of the period are the faultlessly executed inscriptions in hard stone, and skillful metal and faience work. Demotic, the third and last form of Egyptian writing, gradually came into common use during this time.

Under King Wehemibre Necho II, 610–595 B. C., the forerunner of the modern Suez Canal was built, a waterway between the Nile and the Red Sea, which eventually also linked the Mediterranean to the latter.

The first Saite king drove out the Ethiopians, as well as the Assyrians, who had begun their ascendancy in the East during the end-phase of the preceding dynasty, briefly occupying Memphis. Large colonies of foreign settlements developed. This now controlled influx of new elements contributed greatly to the prosperity of the country. The only town in Egypt from which Greek traders could deal was Naucratis, founded in the Delta in about 590 B. C. The only coins ever minted in ancient Egypt came from here. Many Greek mercenaries were now in the pay of the kings of Egypt.

In 525 B. C. all of Egypt fell to the Persian king Cambyses of Dynasty XXVII. The country became a satrapy for the Persian Empire until the latter's defeat in 490 B. C. by the Greeks at Marathon. Revolts against the foreign yoke, albeit on the whole unsuccessful, were staged on and off. Egypt recovered her independence for some sixty years, only to be under the domination of the Persian Empire once more, from 343-332 B. C., this period being considered the last Dynasty (XXXI). It ended with the arrival of Alexander the Great who, under the prevailing circumstances, was considered a deliverer from occupation. The Persian domination seems not to have been, however, one of harsh treatment of the population. Persian influence throughout this rule left very few cultural traces in the country. By the time of Cambyses the waterway, built in the Saite Period, had silted up. As it was important for communications between the capital on the Persian Gulf and the Egyptian satrapy, it was restored in 518 B. C., an event commemorated in stelae set up along the banks. After another silting-up, it was once more restored in Ptolemaic times.

Alexander of Macedonia was formally installed as pharaoh in the temple of Ptah at Memphis during his brief stay in Egypt, having made all the customary sacrifices to the Memphite gods. As his capital on Egyptian soil he founded the sea-board city of Alexandria, soon to become the focal point of Greek culture, as well as international trade. Traditional art styles continued alongside an art schooled in the Greek manner, particularly in terms of naturalistic tendencies, until the end of the Ptolemaic Period.

On Alexander the Great's death in 323 B. C., his successor and half-brother sent as satrap to Egypt the military commander, Ptolemy Lagos, who, in 305 B. C., became king of Egypt and took the additional name of Soter (Saviour), founding the Ptolemaic Dynasty of fifteen kings bearing the name Ptolemy, which ended with Cleopatra VII Philopator. Under the Ptolemies, Egypt's civilization flourished once more. The political administration was run along Greek lines. Greek was the official language, with all three Egyptian scripts in use on religious and secular texts. Greek and Asiatic gods were introduced into religion, including the cult of Serapis, a deity bearing the characteristics of both Osiris and the Greek god Zeus. The Serapeum of Alexandria was considered one of the Wonders of the Ancient World. The principal Egyptian deities nevertheless retained their place of importance, a state of affairs carefully fostered by the kings. Many of the great sanctuaries were reconstructed or built during the period. Ptolemais, a city in Upper Egypt, was founded. Under Ptolemy II, the museum and famous library at Alexandria were built, the waterway between the Red Sea and the Nile reopened, and the translation of the Old Testament into Greek carried out. The key to the deciphering of hieroglyphics, the Rosetta Stone, was a decree in honour of Ptolemy V, its text written in 196 B. C. in hieroglyphics, Greek and Demotic. This king was a particular benefactor of the native temples.

By the end of the first century B. C., Egypt lost her acquired Asiatic Empire. Control of government began to weaken due to increasing dynastic squabbles. Rome's interest in Egyptian affairs took on dangerous proportions, and under the reign of Ptolemy XII from 80–50 B. C., she actively intervened. Egypt became, for all practical purposes, a dependent of Rome, and eventually one of her provinces after the sea battle at Actium in 30 B. C. Following this occurred the suicide of Cleopatra and the killing of her and Caesar's son, nominally Ptolemy XV Caesarion, by order of Octavian.

"Copt" is an abbreviation from the Greek "Aigyptios," a term used to describe the early Christian native inhabitants of Egypt. At the time of the Moslem conquest, the majority of people living in the Nile Valley were Christians. The Arabs had further transformed the name for those of pure Egyptian stock (versus Graeco-Roman settlers and their descendants) into Qibt, from which form the term entered into European usage in the 16th Century A. D. The historic period of Egypt from the 4th to the 7th centuries A. D. is also referred to as the Coptic.

Furthermore, the term defines the rites of the original Christian church in Egypt. Approx. 10 per cent of the present day population still adhere to this belief.

Coptic represents the last phase of the pharaonic language, adding a vocabulary in keeping with the realities of religious and administrative needs of the time. Instead of hieroglyphics, the Greek alphabet was used in the Coptic language, with a further seven specific characters added. Numerous translations from the Old and New Testaments, works of the Greek Fathers and many more, exist mainly on parchment, but also papyrus, stone or ostraka. Coptic was written and spoken up to the thirteenth century A. D. and until very recently it remained the liturgical language of the Egyptian Christians.

Egypt remained politically part of the Roman and Byzantine Empires until the Moslem conquest of A. D. 641.

Coptic art developed from the early monastic communities which, in themselves, were the greatest contribution of the Copts to Christianity. The assimilation of Graeco-Roman and Byzantine elements in later Coptic art led to the frequent mingling of pagan motives with orthodox Christian subjects.

While little architecture remains from Coptic Egypt, ikons, statues and particularly countless decorative tapestry and embroidery fragments were found, testifying to an astonishingly rich and vigorous art style.

50) COPTIC TEXTILES

Of the many thousand textiles found, preserved intact in the dry hot climate, only a few can be dated with some accuracy. All those extant date from the third to the eighth centuries A. D. Roundels and squares of such textiles were sewn into tunics.

The discovery of such a great body of textiles from this period is due to the change of burial customs and gradual abandonment of earlier methods from the fourth century A. D. on. Dead persons were now buried in their daily clothing of two tunics and a cloak. Sometimes, wrappings were hung around the body as a grave cloth. In this, an ancient funerary custom was followed: from early dynastic times onwards, a length of burial cloth was included in the tomb for use in the after-life, inscribed with date of use and other details.

The bulk of the extant textiles are of tapestry work; embroidered examples are rare. Throughout the centuries of production, style, themes, and techniques were subject to changes.

One illustration is of a tapestry from the fifth C. A. D., done in a decorative style of great beauty. The red eagle, wings stylized in their position, holds a ribbon in its beak, the terminals of which are formed by the beaks of two birds. This latter motif is related to the "Animal Style" art of Iran.

The other tapestry square is from the sixth C. A. D., and has as its subejct matter the favourite theme of the birth of Aphrodite. The figures, in a near-humorous style of rendering, within the centre, show all the basic elements of clumsy proportions, with great bulging eyes. Nereids in boats, fish and birds surround the major event, and a guilloche border "frames" it all.

As elsewhere during Graeco-Roman times, subjects most favoured were of ancient Greek origin, becoming more and more transformed in Coptic art as time went on. Outside this artistic area, little of such themes was found on Egyptian objects elsewhere, so that the existing Coptic examples are doubly intriguing.

FLINT TOOLS AND WEAPONS

Knowledge of man's antiquity is intimately bound up with the recorded discoveries of various types of primitive tools and weapons of flint used. The form of these prehistoric relics varies within the several phases of the Stone Age. In ancient Egypt, flint was found in great quantity as nodules in the limestone of the Nile Valley or actually on the surface where the limestone had eroded. Until the coming of metal, flint was, together with stone the raw material most commonly used for tools and weapons of the Palaeolithic to the Neolithic Ages (except for the preference for obsidian and harder rocks for tool grinding during the latter period.) Great skill was evidenced in the utilization of the material to its fullest by techniques of chipping, flaking, and often polishing. Flint remained in use for particular purposes even after copper was introduced. It continued to be employed for centuries for the grinding of stone vessels, carving of ivory and for sickle blades. During dynastic times, ritual significance was attached to the use of flint knives for the slaughtering and dismembering of sacrificial animals. Flint is chemically a quartz, hard but brittle. It can be easily flaked in any direction. Also used was an inferior type of flint, chert.

Bifacial flaking was customary in Egypt as long as tools and weapons of flint remained in use, i.e. certainly up to the New Kingdom. The greatest accomplishment in the manufacture of ripple-flaked knives was achieved during the Nakada II Period. Some of these knives were equipped with handles of carved ivory and gold, and, consequently, were highly treasured objects.

The process of making flint tools was developed during the Pleistocene period. The basic method was to modify a block of the hard material so as to be used as a separate tool, or to chip off flakes from it. This primary block, or core, had either a uniform texture making the removal of flakes easier, or a coarse, uneven texture which resulted in irregular features. The second process was the retouching. Both stages in the manufacture of flint tools and weapons were carried out with a stone hammer, or one made of wood, bone, or antler. Flakes removed from the flint core were divided into three general categories: 1. flakes; 2.

blades which were long and narrow flakes, with the length being at least twice the width; and 3. bladelets: blades of ½″ width or less. From the early 3rd millenium, the plough was used in Egypt, made of hard wood to which a large flint blade was attached.

The oldest, if crude, handaxes were found mainly in Africa. Usually large, bifacially worked core tools, these are the diagnostic implements of the Lower Palaeolithic tool industries in Africa, Europe and South West Asia. The term is somewhat of a misnomer as it is not an axe at all but apparently was an all-purpose tool. Shapes are classified, based on the ratio of length of width at different points in the tool, as well as the thickness and the flaking technique used, as: cordiform, oval, triangle, or Micoqulian. The appearance of axes and adzes in great numbers took place during the early Neolithic Period. In this period falls also the general use of pressure flaking for retouching of objects.

Among the tools of the early Neolithic period are sickle blades for reaping wild or domesticated cereals, as well as, and predominantly, knive blades of many different purposes, lengths, and widths. Sickle blades were hafted into bone or wood handles. Blades were either tools in themselves or the blanks from which burins or scrapers were manufactured, in what is termed the "r oburin technique." Sickle blades are often heavily denticulated on their working edge.

The exact function of the many finds of dibbles is not known. They were possibly used for making holes in the ground for seeding, or they may have been used to enlarge holes in wood after the employment of the gimlet, or for boring ivory, etc. A great number of different grinding tools were also made of flint, in a variety of forms and for many purposes.

Axeheads, some of greenstone, were tied with leather thongs to the haft. In some cases, the thongs still exist. Polishing was done with the aid of sand and water from later Neolithic times onwards. Polishing of tools and weapons was done as a means to further modify the implements, particularly those for grinding. Greenstone is a loose term compris g jade, jadeite, nephrite, olivine, serpentine, chloromelamite. All varieties of these rocks were used by ancient peoples interchangeably, mainly for high quality ceremonial axes, figurines, etc. "Celt" is a 19th century A.D. term which has largely become obsolete (excepting some particular types of axe, adze or hoe heads) because it was based on a mistranslation from the original Latin.

Bows and arrows were used for hunting, as a sport, for obtaining food supplies, as well as in a defensive struggle against the lion, hippopotamus, etc. Big game was forced into southern Egypt during the 4th millenium B.C., having been extensively hunted before then. A favourite pastime for kings and nobles was the big game hunt with bow and arrow as testified to in many surviving descriptions from historical times. At all times, temples had to be supplied with sacrificial animals, shot or trapped by especially appointed hunter-police. Hunting down an animal was also considered a magical act: as the arrow penetrated its victim, silent spells were cast against actual or potential enemies, public and private, also against foreigners, demons and ill-meaning magicians.

Other than pictorial representations, arrowheads are generally the only evidence of archery, since bows and hafts rarely survived the passing of time. Arrows were tipped with flint or chert, as well as with bone barbs. (1a)

1a)
CHERT ARROWHEAD
     Leaf-shaped type with denticulated edges and unifacial bevelling, flat underside. Chisel-ended butt was carefully flaked and possibly also put to some use.

FLINT ARROWHEAD
     Hollow-based type. Of the rounded wing tips, one is slightly longer than the other. Edges are straight on slightly convex sides. Bevelling is bifacial.

CHERT ARROWHEAD
     Barbed and tanged type, with bifacial flaking and denticulated edges.

FLINT ARROWHEAD
     With unifacial bevelling and flat underside.

All: C.

POTTERY

Badarian vessels of the Early Predynastic Period have never been surpassed in their evenness of shape, regularity, and remarkably thin walls. These household utensils were also used as grave offerings (I). They are open bowls without true rims, hand built-up without the aid of the wheel. Prefiring polish was given the vessels by means of quartz pebbles. The outer rim and upper interior were carbonized by firing the vessels in inverted position; sometimes the whole pot was blackened. Also characteristic of this period were pottery drinking vessels with a ripple burnish, the latter achieving a decorative effect as well as rendering the vessel more watertight (XXXII). The shape of the bottom of many vessels required them to have a separate stand.

The period following the Badarian saw a great development in shapes and sizes of pottery while the carbonising of the rim remained essentially the same, unchanged for centuries.

During Nakada I (Amratian) appeared the first examples of painted geometric designs, in white or cream on polished red clay vessels, with a few representations of animals, plants or figure subjects.

The Egyptian generic name for vase is Henu, but a great number of name-variants existed according to the purpose of the object.

During Nakada II (Gerzean) for pottery making, the clay deposits in the wadis of the eastern desert near Aena (Qena) were utilised for the purpose, rather than Nile mud. Aena remains to this day the centre of a thriving pottery industry. Predominantly geometric patterns were still used in a more varied form from those previously. Characteristic of the Gerzean decorated ware (XXXII) are the bulbuous pots, some as high as 2 feet, intended to contain beer, wine, or dry goods.

On many of these pots, wavy lines representing water, water creatures, ibexes, bulls, antelopes, goats, and highly stylised mountains, occur. Some of the animals thus represented were found in graves from post-Badarian times; presumably they were credited with some divine power, hence their frequent depiction on pottery. Lines of long-legged, long-necked birds, identified with flamingoes or ostriches, referred to in later Egyptian texts as Niw, are a common theme on such pots.

The standard, together with the pictorial representation of the Great Mother, or fetish goddess, with arms above her head in an apparent orant position, were the most often used subjects on these vessels. The type of this goddess corresponds to the painted clay female figurines made during Nakada I. Insigniae of a number of male gods are also recognizable on many vessels. These objects are, in some ways, the main identification source for the oldest gods and divinities of Egypt, yet their iconography has, regrettably, not been made a subject for intensive study by specialists.

Another typical pottery product of Nakada II is the squat vase with wave design ledge handles and a red or purple on buff, evenly distributed spiral design and four parallel "water lines" between handles and neck. In later periods, stone vessels were modelled on this type. Some of these unpolished, purple on buff jars were used to contain honey, and called Djadjau.

During the Archaic or Thinite Period, i.e. Dynasties I and II, the wheel began to be used for producing pottery. Called Behep, it was rotated by the left hand, while the right hand modelled the surface of the vessel. From tomb scenes we know of the use of a high kiln with the same phonetic name-value as that for earth (Ta).

After the early Dynastic Period, native Egyptian pottery showed little progress in new forms or decoration. The decorated ware disappeared; the black-and-red pots which throughout predynastic times were so commonly in favour, were no longer made in Egypt proper. They continued to be used in Nubia; their type reappeared in Nubian pan-grave burial sites in Egypt during the Second Intermediate Period. Native pottery was largely replaced by stone vessels; import ware became a major part of ceramic vessels in use. Extensive finds of foreign painted pottery have been made, dating from the end of the Predynastic Period through the Old and Middle Kingdoms (except during dynasties II and III). From the Second Intermediate Period on, Minoan, Cypriot and Syrian pottery was found.

Famous among the imports were the many graceful examples of Tell el-Yahudiyeh ware, in particular juglets. The ware is named after the site (Leontopolis) in Lower Egypt where

31

traces of habitation go back to the Middle Kingdom. It became important during the Hyksos reign from which time the pottery is dated. The Hyksos, who ruled also over Palestine, established trade relations with other Mediterranean countries, accounting for the appearance of the Yahudiyeh ware in enormous numbers.

During the New Kingdom gaily decorated vases began to be made, often with floral motifs. In style and craftsmanship they cannot be ranked with the masterpieces of the predynastic potter's products, however. Glazed pottery does not occur in ancient Egypt until the sixth century B. C. after the commercial settlement at Naucratis near Sais brought Greek potters to the country.

Terracotta, aside from its use in brick-making, for pottery and household utensils, had not been explored as a medium by Egyptian artists until they were influenced by Greece and the Hellenistic world. Clay portrait heads, representing people of many different ethnic groups, have been found at Memphis, dating from the seventh century B. C. Widespread utilization of clay took place in Ptolemaic and Roman times, particularly for figurines as votive offerings, household images etc.

From the Roman Period on, there appeared to be a general use of terracotta oil lamps. With very few exceptions, these lamps were of a type common throughout all contemporary Mediterranean areas. The most frequently produced type was of lentoid shape with a top centre hole for filling with oil and a nozzle hole for the wick. These lamps were mould-made in two pieces, usually bearing the potter's mark, a letter or a geometrical design, at the base. Less common were the loop-handled lamps, decorated with a frog or a mythological animal. They date mostly from the third and fourth centuries A. D. Lamps of clay continued to be made into the late Coptic Period (47).

47) CLAY OIL LAMP
of buff-ware, almond shape, with a wide wick-hole and almond-shaped ring base. The handle is broken off. On the top end is a relief head of Silenus with a long beard, bushy moustache and eyebrows in one continuous line. Around his forehead are thick braids of hair, which also reach from above to below the ears. The snub-nosed features are superbly modelled. The sloping undersides of the nozzle have a ribbed design.. C.

Classification of this object was, in greater part, particularly as to provenance, made by Dr. Warda Sussmann, .Dept. of Antiquities, Jerusalem in "Herodian lamps in the Clark Collection," vs14.

I) BADARIAN BURIAL

The body, in flexed position in a shallow grave, is surrounded by a number and varied shapes of the black-rim ware with extremely thin walls, as well as flint tools. Skin and hair are still adhering to body, head respectively. From bodies found in cemeteries of Upper Egypt such as this, it is evident that the typical Egyptian of the time was slim of build, with delicate features. Clay and ivory figures from the period would indicate that the men wore beards and large penis sheaths, linking them ethnically to the Libyans.

II) FIGURE OF IBIS — GILDED WOOD AND BRONZE

From Dynasty XXVI, the ibis here represents Thoth-Dehuty, head of the great ogdoad of creator-gods at Hermopolis. The sanctuary to Thoth in that town was extremely popular during Ptolemaic times, and continued as a pilgrimage site into the Roman era. The ibis was venerated as the incarnation animal of the god of learning and wisdom, inventor of science and the arts, and scribe of the gods and god of the scribes. The catacombs at Hermopolis, north east of Tell el-Amarna in Upper Egypt stretch for hundreds of miles and can still be visited. Ibises were carefully bandaged, sometimes with consummate skill (III) and put into clay jars or therimorphic coffins to be buried.

Of the three kinds of ibis which existed in ancient Egypt, only one, known as Hib, was sacred to Thoth. Its body was white with a black head and tail. It still survives in the marshes of upper Sudan. The hieroglyph for "to shine" is a representation of an ibis with a brown plumage and crest.

The ibis was often shown, as here, together with the goddess of justice and truth, Ma'at. Imhotep, architect of Dynasty III and builder of the Step Pyramid of King Djoser, was deified in the Late Period as a great sage and god of healing, and ibis mummies were offered to him. Approx. one million of them were found, mostly contained in pottery jars, at his tomb at Sakkara. This first known genius and vizier to the king, later revered also as an astronomer and writer, was associated by the Greeks with their own god of medicine, Asklepios; they called him Imhouthes. His hieroglyphic name translates as "he who gives contentment."

1

III) IBIS WITHIN MUMMY WRAPPINGS

This is a superb example of the care sometimes lavished on the mummy wrapping of the bird incarnate of the god of writing, Thoth, and the deified Imhotep, believed to be a miracle healer in later times. The cemeteries at Hermopolis, cult centre of Thoth, stretching for hundreds of miles and still to be seen, contained many thousands of remains of the white ibis with black tail and head.

Superimposed upon the wrappings is a representation of Nefer-tum, member of the Memphite triad of gods, son of Ptah, who the Greeks identified with Hephaestus, thus associating Nefer-tum with their Prometheus. His name, "Atum-the-Younger" indicates that he was thought to be the rejuvenated Atum who sprang from the divine lotus, asylum of the sun during the night. As here, his attribute is the lotus stalk; he is identified with Lower Egypt.

For a time, he had replaced Imhotep as the god of medicine, hence his association with the ibis. He is the son also of Sekhmet, who sends sickness to the people of Egypt, but who was also considered the goddess of doctors.

Many medical specialists worked in ancient Egypt: the "nose-doctor," "doctor of the abdomen," "eye-doctor of the palace," "he who knows the inner juices of the body," and many more. The equivalent of the modern plaster cast were bandages dipped in glue-like resin. Slices of raw meat were applied as pressure-bandage and blood-clotting ferment. Circumcision, at puberty, was practised, and may have been of Egyptian origin. Above one such scene the inscription reads: "It will do you good!" The hieroglyph for heart looks like an oval pot with two handles shaped like ears (the auricles or upper chambers of the heart).

IV) TRIAD OF KING MEN-KAU-RE AND GODDESSES

Made of schist, with traces of colouring, this is one of four complete groups of the same theme found in the Valley Temple of the third pyramid at Giza. The features of the goddesses are in the likeness of the queen. The king is supported by Hathor on one side and by the figure personifying the nome or administrative district of Diapolis Parva, by means of the emblem atop her head. A number of other such triads showing this king with two females supporting him, found in fragmentary state, would indicate that there was one such group made for each district. The inscription on the base of the sculpture indicates that Hathor has " . . . given you all good offerings of the South forever." Statuary showing the wives supporting their husbands with their arms around them was first made for Men-Kau-Re. It became the standard composition for many sculptures in ensuing dynasties. Statues of this king reveal a less aloof personality than his predecessors' of Dynasty IV. In Egyptian folklore he lived as a pious king who undid the wrongdoings of the builders of the two greater pyramids, Chufu and Khafre.

The king wears the White Crown of Upper Egypt, ceremonial beard held in place by straps and, as do both goddesses, the emblematic staves of office in his hands. His left leg is advanced in accordance with artistic dictates. The all-over pleated kilt of royalty, with its protruding tab is called shendyt.

V) SERVANT FIGURE OF THE POTTER NE-INPU-KAU AT WORK — DYNASTY VI, OLD KINGDOM

A great deal of paint still on this limestone figure helps to create a very realistic effect of the actual features of a member of the underprivileged class, with his high cheekbones, slightly tilted nose, and resigned expression. The squatting position is still the custom in many Eastern countries. The man is shown turning the potter's wheel with the left, and the piece he is fashioning with the right hand. The three up-side down arranged pots are of the type illustrated in XXXII.

This is a far cry from representations of the well-fed men of the aristocratic or upper classes Ne-inpu-kau might have worked for, who, in any event, were shown in idealised versions of themselves. This artistic limitation was not deemed necessary when depicting common people. Thus portraits of servant figures from the Old King-dom afford us an undiluted, if some-what sad, look at another aspect of life in "the two lands."

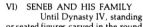

VI) SENEB AND HIS FAMILY

Until Dynasty IV, standing or seated figures carved in the round were the basic forms of sculpture. Seneb, court tutor of Dynasty VI, head of the royal textile mills and an official with numerous titles, whose wife was entitled to be called prin-cess, posed a unique problem for the sculptor by his dwarf-figure. The conventional arrangement of the wife's arm around her husband in such a group is retained, and, by Seneb's squatting on a bench, sym-metry achieved by placing the fig-ures of his children beneath it. With a head disproportionally large, Seneb appears to be the same height as his wife in this group. In this "genre" style sculpture of the Old Kingdom, the idealising tendencies are not in conflict with the unusual physical appearance of the owner of the tomb. The cubic conception of statuary, a hallmark of the period, is admirably brought out. Seneb's titles are enumerated on the bench, while on the wall of the niche behind the group are listed his possessions. Seneb's short-cropped hair is sculp-ted in staggered circles on top of the head and down to the nape of the neck. His wife's simple wig displays a little of her own hair beneath it. As was customary in Egyptian painting, the flesh of females was usually ren-dered lighter (yellow) than that of men; this extended to mummy wrappings. Here, apparently, the colour has been lost from the bodies of Seneb's wife and daughter, while his body and that of his son retain their original colour. The children are shown with their forefingers held to the mouth: this and the sidelock make up the hieroglyph for infancy or youth. The names of the children, also carved into the plinth, are com-pounded with those oF King Red-jedef and King Khufu of Dynasty IV, for whose funerary cults their father acted as one of the priests.

III

VII) LIMESTONE RELIEF OF
OFFERING-BEARERS
From the tomb of Nenk-
hefta-ka, a priest during Dynasty
VI, this fragment of a relief carving,
with vivid colouring still extant,
shows the rendering of the human
figure in ancient Egyptian art of relief and painting. The frontally
placed eye in the profile face has its
echo in the arrangement of the
shoulders. Thumbs of both hands on
the second man are on the same
sides. Two of the multitude of vessel
types are shown, containing perhaps
ointments or spices.

VIII) LIMESTONE SUNK RELIEF
OF A PRINCESS
This fragment of a relief
showing the family of Akhenaten
worshipping is a superb example of
the sculptor's workmanship when
employed on a royal commission.
The head is elongated in the style of
early Amarna mannerism. The eye
is still shown in front view in a profile face. The depth of the carving
varies, giving the head some degree
of plasticity. The princess Merit-
aten wears the sidelock of youth
held in place by some jewellery
clasp. Her own hair is just visible
under the wig covering it. Her hand
holds the sistrum. The light red
colour is modern.

IX) BLOCK STATUE OF HORI, PRIEST OF MONTH

In continuous use from the Middle Kingdom to end-Ptolemaic times was this type of squatting figure. It was introduced into statuary of private persons and placed in temple niches. The statue of Hori is of end-XXVth Dynasty—beginning of Dynasty XXVI, the last period of great sculpture, when Old and Middle Kingdom examples were copied, based on thorough studies of antiquities. Characteristic of this time is the superb surface finish as seen on this schist sculpture. The wig is especially finely executed, and the hieroglyphs are ornamentally worked. The cuboid form allows for inscriptions on all four sides. The text on the front of the statue contains an offering formula and invocation of the Late Period war-god Month. This type of figure was never meant to be viewed from an angle, since it was not set out in the open, but rather formed an essential part of the structure. It is to be seen either full-face or full-profile. The arms placed outside the cubist form is not a common feature in such "block" statues; Hori's right hand holds the emblematic stave of office. The very short beard connecting chin and folded arms works to emphasise the compactness of the cloaked figure.

X) KA OF KING HOR

Representing the spiritual aspect of the son and co-regent of Amen-em-het III, this religious cult statue of wood was found within the wooden shrine shown here. It retains some of its original grey paint and gilding and invokes that intangible spirit which the Egyptians believed continued to exist after the physical death of a person, and which it was necessary to provide with access to eternal life, i. e. kept content and nourished lest a second, final death occur. One of the few remaining wooden sculptures, it was once draped with a loin cloth. In its pose (forward-striding, upward gazing, with idealised features) it recalls statuary of the Old Kingdom. However, the slender and somewhat elongated form belongs to an art whose sophistication foreshadows mannerism of a later period. An unusual feature is the fact that head, torso and left leg are carved in one piece, while the remaining parts are separately carved and attached by tenons.

The statue is carved with the ceremonial beard of royalty and a splendidly carved wig cover surmounted by the hieroglyphic sign for KA = life and afterlife. The figure's eyes are of glass inlay.

Xa) LIMESTONE STATUE OF AMEN-HOTEP I, SECOND KING OF DYANSTY XVIII

Seated on a cubic throne, the king wears the royal Nemes, green and yellow striped, in which the hole for the now missing uraeus is visible. The black ceremonial beard is attached by leather straps which, however, do not continue realistically behind the ears. He wears the overall-pleated kilt of royalty, the Shendyt. Name and prenomen of the king, in full official form, cover the front surface of the throne and top and front of the plinth. Around the tips of ears and eyelids, the red guidelines of the sculptor can be made out.

CONTINUATION OF Xa

As was the case for kings of the next four centuries, Amen-hotep I had his sepulchre built into the rock of Western Thebes, in favour of the pyramids of preceding ears. He was buried in the oldest royal tomb at Thebes. In the later New Kingdom, he became the deified patron of the Theban necropolis, one of the divine guardians, together with his mother Ahmes-nefer-tari.

Amen-hotep I and his successor extended the southern border of Egypt beyond the third Cataract, and rebuilt fortresses dating from the Middle Kingdom in the area.

XI) PAINTED LIMESTONE SUNK RELIEF OF SMENKH-KA-RE AND MERIT-ATEN

Both royal personages wear the uraeus on the brow, the ousekh, and transparent gowns. As often in Amarna art, the custom of painting women's flesh in a lighter tone is here discarded. However, the arrangement of torso relative to the whole body is more anatomically accurate than in other periods of painting and relief.

A scene of marital tenderness, the bare-footed queen holds out mandrake fruits and a lotus bud to her husband; the left hand clasping more lotus buds. After the queen's death, Smenkh-ka-re, half-brother of Akhenaten, married one of her sisters.

The object is thought to have been a decorative panel to be fitted into the mud-brick wall of a palace (versus tomb reliefs). Stylistic features of later Amarna times are obvious but in a very modified manner (elongation of head and neck of Merit-aten). The portrait of the queen is of distinct similarity to others known to be of her. The artist has taken more elaborate care over the figure of the king. The wig with its streamers, the ribbed double sash on his kilt, and the sandals. It seems that he had legs of differing lengths, making necessary the use of a supporting walking-stick, far too long to have been a sceptre or similar, which in any case would not be part of a private scene such as this.

Sometimes called "Promenade in the Garden," this relief emanates a mood of personal experience of a tender relationship. Elegance and poetic tone are elements that created this immensely pleasurable scene.

XII) BROWN QUARTZITE HEAD OF NEFER-TITI

Like many others, this unfinished object was found in a sculptor's studio at Tell el-Amarna. During the reign of Akhenaten the composite statue was invented, enabling specialists to perfect their skill in sculpting one particular part to be assembled with the other components. This unique and clever solution to achieve maximum quality with minimum time of development did not, however, survive the time of "the heretic king."

The sculpture represents an idealised version of the queen. The painted guidelines for the sculptor, as well as the outline for eyes, eyebrows and placing of the headdress help to give this un-finished masterwork of approximately life-size a haunting quality.

XIII) LIMESTONE STELA OF MEKY MONT

In the tradition of funerary stelae, the deceased is seated next to his wife Neb-m-ushat on a high-backed double chair. The blue background is an artistic feature of Dynasty XVIII. The traditional artistic distinction between colours of flesh for male and female is observed. Both wear a short kilt and a transparent, longer garment over it. The woman wears the strapless gown called Kalasiris. An interesting detail is the raised platform on which the chair is placed; it's lion paw legs are not set into the usual protective metal sheated cylinders to keep them off the ground. Meky Mont raises a sacred blue lotus flower to his face. On top, two Udjat eyes flank a SHEN sign (eternity).

The table is laden with the usual food offerings of fruit, bread, legs of beef, and so on, while the brother of the deceased pours a libation over it. The funerary formula below invites Osiris "Lord of Abydos, great god, sovereign of eternity" to grant Meky "oxen, fowl, every good pure offering by which the god lives."

XIV) BRONZE STATUE OF QUEEN KAROMAMA, LIBYAN DYNASTY

The small statue was made by order of a high official for her chapel at Karnak of the consort of King Takelothis II (837–813 B. C.) Gold, silver and electrum were used for inlay of the Broad Collar necklace of floral design, and the Rishi (feather) pattern of the dress. The sleeves are of a type worn by a king some four hundred and fifty years earlier (23). The multi-plaited coiffure, with the Buto cobra, personal king of gods and queens, is surmounted by the now empty modius which held the two-feathered ibes-crown. Karamomama's hands held either two sistra or a sistrum and a sceptre.

From the time when members of the formerly traditional foes of Egypt, the Libyans, sat on her throne, comes little if any monumental work. The period's artists excelled instead in small-scale work of unsurpassed quality, bronzes and jewellery. Figures of bronze were inlaid with gold or silver, electrum, semi-precious stones, glasses, or a layer of gold leaf to give an illusion of life and colour to the bronze.

Perhaps slightly too elongated in the proportions of the lower part, this piece was considered by its purchaser (and translator of the hieroglyphs, Champollion) in 1829 as the most stunningly beautiful work of its kind.

XV) GREEN SLATE STATUE OF PRINCE HAWARA, KUSHITE (XXVth) DYNASTY

The quality of artistic ability and achievement during the Ethiopian Dynasty excelled that of the prior four hundred years. The superior technical skill evidenced in this case is purely Egyptian, but done under the influence of the rude vigour of the southern conquerors, then on the throne of Egypt. It brought about a realism in sculpture of unprecedented quality. Wide cheekbones, a full mouth and flat nose and very rounded skull are an ethnic characteristic in sculpture depicting the ruling house of Dynasty XXV, to judge by the recurrence of the facial type. Realism such as showing the sagging body with its fat folds is one of the most outstanding features of the art of the period. Seated in an unique pose, the sculpture is rendered with keenly observed accuracy of the various elements of the body. Deep grooves running from nostrils to chin complete the picture of old age. Hawara was the steward of the sacerdotal princess Amen-ardis.

XVa) SMALL DIORITE OINTMENT VASE

Under 2" high, this tiny masterwork of a stonecarver from Dynasty III or IV is a compelling example of the highly developed aesthetics in the production of utilitarian objects. Lug-handled and with a flat rim, the superbly proportioned jar has a residue of ointment on the inner walls. C. 605

XVI) VASE

Alabaster — "Onyx marble" with dark veining — flat rim below top to fit lid onto. An example of the high degree of aesthetics employed in the fashioning of utilitarian objects. (C. 608)

XVII) CLAY MOULD FOR THE UDJAT AMULET
Many distinct traditions for the legent of the "Sacred Eye of Horus" exist. Horus was originally the king-god, warrior-god and god of Heaven of Heliopolis—his eye identified with the sun and moon. As RE he later became identified with the sun-god: the solar-eye was attributed to him and the lunar-eye to Horus. Seth, god of Darkness, snatched away Horus' eye. Found in pieces by Thoth and restored, it was given the name UDJAT = "that which is sound." C.

XVIII) FLAT FAIENCE FIGURE OF BES — DYNASTY XXI
With the figure of the infant Horus in his left arm and a baboon crouching between his bandy legs, this object was the terminal of a mirror handle. The lower part of it would have been carved with a magiçal formula to protect the whole family by means of such a figure. In this aspect, Bes was the bringer of happiness to the home as a whole. His function was to protect against evil spirits and dangerous beasts such as scorpions, snakes, crocodiles and lions. His image was often placed atop the figure of the infant Horus in the so-called Cippi of Horus, i. e. small stelae.

XIX) ANUBIS ON A GOLDEN SHRINE — FROM THE TREASURY-ENTRANCE OF THE TOMB OF TUT-ANKH-AMUN

The figure is of black-varnished wood, with gilded details, silver claws, eyes of alabaster and obsidian. When found, it had wrapped around it and knotted under the chin a fringed linen "shirt" with painted hieroglyphic inscriptions. Linen scarves were made specifically for the wrapping of statues of the god. Anubis here represented the king in his transformation after death, as he was believed to supervise and perform the rites of Osiris, who the king was to become himself. His bushy tail extending down to the bottom of the shrine, the animal is "The Embalmer of Anubis" as a black god with the head of a young dog, because black was considered the colour of rebirth.

XX) MUMMY CASE OF KA-TEB-ET. MUSICIAN-PRIESTESS OF AMUN AT THEBES — PTOLEMAIC

The headpiece is of cartonnage with a gilded face, while the hands are of wood, adorned with actual rings (vs. more usually, painted) of carnelian, lapis lazuli, glass stones. The elaborate wig is covered by a gilded lotus headdress. Huge pale blue faience ear-studs, a Broad Collar necklace and bracelets with the gilded Udjat-amulet, make up the jewellery. Below the women's hands, two painted falcon-headed Horus figures each hold on to a vessel with divine libations. A gilt and painted figure of Isis, attached to the bandages, spreads her protective wings. Beneath her, two priests flank Khepri, the sacred beetle, a powerful amulet which, as a hieroglyph, denotes "to come into being." Finally, a pectoral shows Osiris, god of the dead, in his image as wolf, with ceremonial beard and the royal flagellum.

The piece is a prime example of the care taken with binding and the mummy case per se at the expense of careful mummification of the body itself.

XXI) "FAYUM" MUMMY
PORTRAIT — 3rd CENTURY
A. D.
    A characteristic of these
encaustic wax portraits on wood,
placed over the head of the mummy
under the bandages, is that they invariably portray non-native Egyptians but Greeks, Romans and
sometimes Semites.
    Hot beeswax is added to
corasely ground pigments, resulting
in a rich, luminous colour. Usually
shoulders and upper part of the
chest are shown. The head is always
frontally arranged with a slight turn
to one side. A heavy white streak
runs down the nose. The style here
follows realistic Roman portraiture
of the time.
    "Fayum" (Fayumic) is a
generic term for these mummy portraits; although a great number of
them were found in that area, many
more come from other places.
    The earliest examples are
from the early first century A. D.,
while the greatest number date to
the second and fourth centuries.
They were last made in the fourth
century. It was also during this time
that mummification was more and
more replaced by a simple burial of
the dead in their regular dress.

XXII) CANOPIC JAR OF
MERIT-ATEN
    Of alabaster (calcite), with
inlaid eyes, this is one of four jars
found in a cache in the Valley of the
Kings. The tomb from which they
came contained the pillaged remains
of a king's burial. Originally, the jar
lids were made as part of the funerary equipment for the oldest daughter of Akhenaten and Nefer-titi,
Merit-aten was married to her father's half-brother, Smenkh-ka-re
who was for awhile co-regent and,
briefly Akhenaten's successor.
    Inlay on one eyebrow is
partially lost; that from the other
completely, as is the precious stone
from the wig. Remnants of pigment
on lips and wig are visible. The wig
is the multiplaited type fashionable
in the later New Kingdom, with an
upward cut from the nape of the
neck. Because of the distinct Nubian
features of the face, the lid has at
one time been thought to represent
Queen Tiye (of Amenophis III).

XXIIa) SET OF CANOPIC JARS
    The lids represent the protective deities of the embalmed viscera of the wife of Purdjem, High Priest of Amun, Dynasty XXI. Jars and lids are made of faience, and glazed composition respectively. Horus had appointed his sons to guard over the four cardinal points.
    The removal of the internal organs was an essential preliminary to successful mummification. The organs to be embalmed were treated separately wtih natron. The body cavity was afterwards packed, and a plate of leather or, in some instances, a gold leaf covered the sewn-up incision in the left flank. The plate bore on it the powerful Udjat amulet.

XXIII) GROUP
SCARABS OF:
BROWN AGATE — WHITE
CHALCEDONY — STEATITE,
UNGLAZED — TURQUOISE*
BADLY DAMAGED STEATITE
WITHIN GOLD MOUNTING
    Actual sizes.
    *From Dynasty XII, base incised with R-hpr-k = Ra-kheper-ka, Senwosret I. Turquoise was mined in the Sinai, in Wadi Magharah and Serabit el-Khadim. Senwosret's name was found there on other objects. The local goddess of the mines was Hathor, called "Mistress of Turquoise." C.
*Published: Alan Rowe, "Egyptian Scarabs," 1936, 2.

XXIV) USHABTI OF RAMESSES IV

Of painted wood, it is inscribed with the magic spell so that the substitute will act when the king is called up for the corvee in the Osirian other-world. In the New Kingdom the text for this spell, from Chapter IV of the "Book of the Dead," usually read as follows: "N. says 'O shabti! If N. is detailed for any tasks to be done there (in the underworld), as a man is bound, namely to cultivate the fields, to flood the banks of the fields (i. e. to water them) and to carry away sand to the east and to the west, then say thou 'Here I am.' " Ramesses IV is represented here carrying a hoe in each hand and wearing the royal striped headdress, Nemes, with the personal god of the king, the Buto cobra, on his brow. Several cartouches, in various registers over the lower part of the ushabti, bear the king's names.

XXV) USHABTI OF TJAI-HER-PA-TA

Made of light green faience, this is from the very end of the Dynastic Period of Egypt. Rare at this time, the modelling is superb. It represents the deceased in Osirian form, with the royal Nemes headdress and ceremonial beard, carrying a hoe in each hand. The incised inscriptions may have been inlaid with some other glass material.

XXVI) HIEROGLYPHS OF COLOURED ENAMEL ON SYCAMORE WOOD

This reproduces a portion of the wooden sarcophagus lid of Djed-Thoth-of'—ankh of Hermopolis, of the fourth century B.C. Some of the inlaid hieroglyphics are missing, as well as some of the vertical lines. The text contains part of Cahpter LXXII of the "Book of the Dead." The French scholar and translator of the hieroglyphics, Champollion, was the most famous of many admirers of this extremely fine example of inlaid hieroglyphics. Ornamentation with inlay of this type dates back to the Old Kingdom, as exemplified in wooden vases, also on an ivory casket from the 1st Intermediate Period, as well as limestone sarcophagi of Dynasty XXVI with enamel inlays.

XXVII) LIMESTONE OSTRAKON

This, a sketch by an artist of the late XVIIIth Dynasty, shows a young woman dancer-acrobat. The black garment has a band decoration of geometric design possibly representing beads. The annular earring seems to disobey the laws of gravity. Richly plaited hair (presumably not a wig or it would tumble off the head in this movement) touches the ground lightly, as do toes and finger tips.

XXVIII) PAPYRUS MAP OF GOLD MINES AND SCHIST QUARRIES

The only known map drawing from ancient Egypt, it dates from Dynasty XX. Portions of it are missing and the remainder is damaged in several parts.

The mountainous zone of Wadi Hammamat along the Eastern Desert where the major gold deposits were located, is shown in pink, the hieratic inscriptions of the captions spell out details. The enclosed white area represents the Temple of Amun and workers' housing. The stela, also white (near the centre) is inscribed to the second king of Dynasty XIX, Sethos I. The well to the left of it is recognisable as the modern Bir el-Hammamat. The route on the lower portion, marked as a rough road by patches of colour, leads to the other chain of mountains from which schist or basalt (Bhni) was mined.

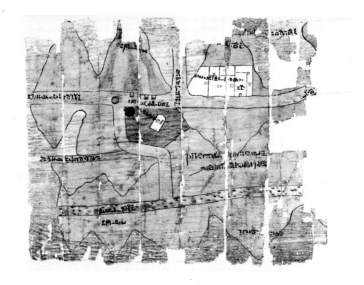

XXIX) BUST OF THE GODDESS HATHOR — PATINATED BRONZE AND GOLD OVER A WOODEN CORE

A garrison of mercenaries from the defeated Sea Peoples during the time of Ramesses III was posted in the site of Beth Shean (modern Israel), from which this piece comes. First the Hyksos of the Second Intermediate Period dominated Palestine and later Egyptian kings ruled the site of Beth Shean, ranging from Tuthmosis III to Ramesses III. Objects pertaining to Egyptian religious practises are, therefore, fairly common archeological finds in the area.

Hathor: her many functions include that of goddess of love, music, dance, jewellery and gold prospectors, patroness of turquoise mines ("Lady of Sinai"), also as the celestial cow who created the world. Particularly, she was the "Queen of the West," protectress of the Theban necropolis in her disguise as a cow with the solar disk between horns above her head. Her role as funerary deity grew to be so specialised that dead persons, formerly called "an Osiris" after the god of the dead, would be referred to as "a Hathor."

Of her many sanctuaries, the temple at Dendera in Upper Egypt was the most important; the sacred marriage of Hathor with Horus took place there. It was also at Dendera that the few religious festivals in which the public was able to participate took place; this was limited to events that involved processions. On the festival celebrating Hathor's birth, New Year's Day, her image was brought onto the terrace of the temple by priestesses to expose it to the rays of the rising sun.

XXIXa) THREE NECKLACES
  Various shapes and colours of faience (1)
  Interspersed with tiny amulets and drop beads of agate and various other stones, this is of carnelian beads (2)
  "Squeezed tube" gold spacers between disks of carnelian (3) all: C.

XXX) SERVANT GIRLS RE-CAPPING PERFUME CONES — PART OF TOMB PAINTING, DYANSTY XVIII
  Guest seated on chairs with the customary animal-leg terminals, "Boatsman's circlet" of flowers in their hair, are being supplied with scented grease to replace that which has already melted down from the cone atop the head. In tomb paintings, the delicately beautiful, transparent garments are sometimes shown suffering from the effect of this "anointment."
  The servant girls here are depicted nude except for a beaded loin belt and also a "Boatsman's circlet." Nudity in Egyptian art is rarely shown and then only for people of particular social groups (prisoners of war, for one).

XXXI) WOODEN COSMETIC SPOON

The slim figure of a young girl, dressed only in her New Kingdom carved and painted wig and the ousekh necklace, holds on to a duck, also adorned with a Broad Collar necklace. Remnants of Nile-green paint are on both parts of this stylistically refined object. The missing lid was hinged to the body of the duck, forming the receptacle.

The craft of the wood carver (especially in toilet articles and particularly unguent spoons) during the New Kingdom achieved heights of refinement and balanced good taste, without the exuberance some of the other arts of the period displayed.

A similar motif of a swimming girl holding on to a gazelle-receptacle was much favoured for these objects. Usually a narrow belt implying beads was strung around the girl's loins, but is missing on the illustrated piece.

XXXII) CYLINDRICAL RED WARE VESSEL

with straight, slightly convex sides and a round bottom, necessitating a separate stand. The stroke burnish was done with a quartz pebble or bone slip. C. (Ascolon)

XXXIII) GERZEAN
DECORATED WARE
    Fashioned in the typical bulbuous shape of this ware, the vessel is decorated with a distinctive circular fringe. As on many such pots, the fringe represents banks of oars on a boat surmounted by two cabins with a standard. In some cases these standards have been identified with the nome-staff of districts from the Dynastic Period. At the prow is often shown what may be the Aloe or the Abessynian banana tree. Rectangular boxes of this ware were also produced, but are rare. The pot, buff-coloured with red decoration, bears below the boats two geometrised plant motifs. The flat lip has a striation design and is in superb proportion to the pear-shaped body of the vessel, with striation-design lug handles and a small, flat base. C. 601.

XXXIV) POLYCHROME
FAIENCE TILE — DYNASTY XX,
APPROX. 1160 B. C.
    From Amarna times to the end of the reign of Ramesses III the height of rich polychrome wall decoration was reached. Tiles with floral and fauna patterns and others adorned palaces and houses, particularly during the Amarna Period. Doorways and balconies were framed with plain blue tiles with the title of the king in white glyphs. They were all made to be set into plastered mud brick.
    This example, from the doorway opening of the first court of the Temple at Medinet Habu attests to the remarkable skill with which the different colour glazes were fused to the composition core. The latter was made of coarse paste, moulded and heat-dried before applying the glaze.
    From the same temple of Ramesses III come tiles depicting other captives and foreigners (Libyans, Syrians, Hittites, Philistines) all, like this, with carefully executed detail of dress and definition of ethnic features. Such details are familiar from many paintings and reliefs.

XXXV) TWO SMALL GLASS COSMETIC OR MEDICINE VESSELS

Clear glass ware for utilitarian purposes produced during Roman times followed in shape that of pottery, metal and stone. The two tiny vessels, one of slightly irregular pear-shape, the other squat, were presumably used for perfume, ointment respectively. The blueish iridescent smaller object has a somewhat disproportionally heavy rim, a feature of a ware by then mass-produced. C. 3671, 3609.

XXXVI) FRAGMENT OF LINEN CLOTH — LATE PREDYNASTIC PERIOD

Two ships of different sizes, painted in black, are moved by helmsmen and crew. These, oars and deck-cabins are painted a reddish colour. The type of boat, arrangement of oars and cabins are of those seen on Gerzean ware pottery of the period (XXXIII).

SLATE PALETTES

The earliest finds of slate palettes came from Badarian graves. They appeared more frequently and became more highly developed during the Gerzean Period, and ceased to be made soon after the commencement of the Dynastic Period.

The earliest known examples were either shapeless, or rectangular with slightly rounded sides. Throughout the period of their manufacture a variety of shapes were incorporated, including trapezoid, round, and shield-shapes. From Nakada I on, animal shapes were gradually introduced including the hippopotamus, hare, monkey, elephant, antelope, fish or double fish, bird or double-bird, Barbary sheep. These first pieces of schist became the most consistent item of funerary equipment of the period, often placed next to the face or hands of the deceased. Eyes of animals represented in these palettes were usually inlaid with ring beads of ostrich egg shell, and sometimes perforated the stone. Because of the flat, utilitarian surface of the palettes, animals were rendered in highly stylized fashion. Miniature sized palettes of rhombic and other shapes were found which had no practical, but probably magical, functions. A special type of predynastic palette, termed "pelta," seems equipped with too narrow a body to have been utilized for grinding, thus presumably was meant for some ritual. Its shape perhaps was evolved from reed boats.

The most popular shape of palette during the Gerzean period was the fish (1a). The fish motif is a recurrent one in Egyptian art from Predynastic—into Christian times, particularly for utilitarian objects.

At the very end of the Predynastic Period, richly decorated palettes, with relief carvings commemorating particular events, were made. Their purpose was ceremonial rather than functional. They were to become the most important historic objects from the time.

With some palettes, the pebbles used for grinding the colour have been found. Many palettes show striation marks resulting from the grinding. Cakes of green malachite, as well as traces of that substance on palettes were also discovered.

1) SLATE PALETTE

end of Late Predynastic Period, approx. 3200 B. C. The rectangular shape with rounded lower sides seems to have been the preferred type towards the end-Gerzean period and the beginning of Dynastic Egypt. The top is of openwork carving representing the front and tail end of a "comb bird" with "feathers" arranged in an upright pattern.

SLATE PALETTE

Gerzean Period, approx. 3400–3200 B. C. The shape, representing the Tilapia Nilotica species of fish, is of the frequently found type. Fins and gillet are incised.

 The malachite which was ground on these palettes was mixed with fat or resin to produce the desired consistency, and applied for the purpose of reducing glare, and to act as germicide. This green paint was also applied between eyes and nose, a custom still practised during Old Kingdom times. The paint is mentioned in offering lists of the period. It is the cosmetic most frequently found in predynastic graves. From the end–Gerzean Period on, the green paint symbolized the sound eye of Horus as mentioned in the Pyramid Texts; from the same period came slate palettes in the shape of the Horus falcon. A tomb painting from the XIIth Dynasty shows a group of Semites trading eye-paint from the governor of the Eastern Desert.

 For the mixing of malachite and fat, shells and large spoons were used from Badarian times onwards. A number of other utensils were, furthermore, required: small leather or cloth bags for storage of the cakes of malachite; plain or carved tusks with holes in the top and leather covers held by leather thongs, in which the precious powder was carried. Small ivory and, later, alabaster vases were also made to store the malachite-based substance. The value of the content of such vessels is borne out by their carefully fitting lids. A vase to hold this cosmetic, carved by an artist of the Badarian culture, is in the shape of a hippopotamus. MALACHITE: green carbonate of copper and the essential raw material in its production, was obtained from the Eastern Desert and, possibly, also imported from Cyprus.

34

LANGUAGE, WRITING

Both the Semitic and Hamitic language groups have given the Egyptian language some words. At least 300 of the former and about 100 of the latter have been identified. Furthermore, a number of words were shared by these different language groups. The principal peculiarity common to the Semitic and the ancient Egyptian languages is that their word-stems consist of (normally) three consonants, in theory unchangeable, with a complicated system of adding internal vowels, which were not written.

The very early occasional contacts with peoples of other countries, as far as Mesopotamia, as well as the fusion of races affected the language development. Certain agricultural terms used in Egypt, for instance, were clearly derived from Sumerian words for corresponding meanings.

The hieroglyphic script (Greek hieros = sacred, glupho = sculpture) after its full development into a continuous narrative at the beginning of dynastic Egypt was retained for almost three thousand years, though not throughout in secular texts, and, at the end confined to a very small circle of learned priests. Originally an offshoot of the older pictorial writing, hieroglyphic script was first used for all purposes, religious and secular, on stelae of stone on temple and tomb walls, often elaborated in detail and beautifully coloured, and on papyrus (XXVI).

Some 700 signs had to be mastered. The illiterate sculptor or painter transferring them onto walls, bases of figures, etc., worked from stock models. To become a scribe meant to study from the age of four for twelve years. Scribes enjoyed a number of privileges, such as tax-exemption. To be a scribe was a prerequisite for embarking upon the career of a high-ranking member of the army, Treasury or at the Palace. Few, but some, scribes were girls. From at least Middle Kingdom times a word existed for female scribe. A grafitto in King Djoser's Pyramid makes sneering reference to the literary efforts of women. Palettes of two of Akhenaten's daughters are extant.

Since Middle Egyptian was considered the classical language, in use for some monumental and literary texts until Graeco-Roman times, pupils of later days learnt a language long dead. The result of this is that much of Egyptian literature handed down is a somewhat garbled version of the original.

Hieroglyphs could be written in either direction, thus allowing for the possibility of a highly decorative arrangement.

Early in dynastic times, certainly from Dynasty V (with some sporadic examples dating as early as the Thinite Period) a much less cumbersome and rapid script developed out of hieroglyphic writing: the hieratic (Greek: hieratikos = priestly, because in Greek times it was used for religious texts only). First written in vertical columns, by Dynasty XII the text was set into horizontal lines, which allowed for a more cursive hand of the writer. It was always written from right to left (39). From the New Kingdom, two distinct versions of this script, one for literary and one for business documents, was used. Black ink and a thin reed brush with frayed end were used for hieratic texts on papyrus. Red ink marked the beginning of a new paragraph, punctuations in literary texts, or particular cereals and the names of evil creatures, since red was considered the colour of evil forces. Rarely carved into stone, hieratic was also written on leather, on potsherds and limestone flakes (ostraka).

Some forty documents only are known to exist written in the so-called abnormal hieratic, a derivative of the business hieratic of the Late Kingdom. These date from the eighth to the sixth centuries B. C.

A new cursive script, used exclusively for secular documents, began first to appear in Lower Egypt of the seventh century B. C. Called demotic (Greek: demotikos = popular) or sometimes enchorial (enkhorios = native). This, too, was written from right to left only. The earliest extant specimens of this form of writing date from the Saite Period. It remained in use until the fifth century A. D.

Throughout, hieroglyphics remained in use for religious texts on monuments and in stone generally.

Ostraka (sing. ostrakon, Greek: shell, sherd): from Old Kingdom to Arab times, these served as cheap writing material for school exercises, for preliminary drawings, for the squaring process the Egyptians applied on rendering the human figure in art (40), for accounts, lists of workmen, letters and all other aspects of daily life. As "sketch-pads" for artists, they usually show

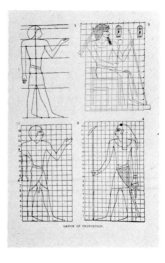

40) CANONS FOR DRAWING THE HUMAN FIGURE
To aid in the delineation of the human figure two methods were used. In the Old Kingdom horizontal lines were made on the surface of the material, the distances between the lines being in fixed or varying ratio in proportion to the size of parts of the body. Whilst from the Middle Kingdom onwards the surface was marked out in small rectangles of equal size, much the same as in the "painting by squares" used by children today.

a much more free and spontaneous style than that of the strictly prescribed art of the finished versions (XXVII). The great number of satirical ostraka show the Egyptian's delight in turning the order of things upside down.

General knowledge of reading and writing hieroglyphics was apparently lost soon after it was superceded by the hieratic and demotic scripts. It was in this latter form of the Egyptian language that the hieroglyphic text on the Rosetta Stone was translated. The presence of a second translation in Greek accompanying the text, enabled scholars to finally decipher hieroglyphics in the eraly 19th century A.D.

39) PART OF THE "RHIND MATHEMATICAL PAPYRUS"

Written in the hieratic script from right to left on horizontal lines, this is from the time of Auserre Apophis I of the Hyksos (XVth) Dynasty, dating to approx. 1600 B. C.

It shows problems concerned with the calculation of areas. From this document (on another part) we know that the value of lead was half that of silver and a quarter that of gold.

"Books" were kept in jars and boxes, carefully rolled. Many private "libraries" were found in Thebes, consisting of magical texts, hymns, folk tales, mythological stories, and others. Priests were the permanent keepers of literary works in temples. Clay bowls with "letters to the dead" in hieratic script were put into tombs as a means of communication between the living and the deceased's "place of residence."

RELIGION

Particular deities of ancient Egypt were elevated to higher status within local cults without affecting the role played by the major gods (28). Gradually, such local deities were assimilated into the Egyptian pantheon, to add to the amalgam of religious beliefs. This resulted in an infinite variety of character and function of deities. In early times, gods were worshipped in the shape of animals or inanimate objects. Early Dynastic kings were considered as the omnipotent god, the god incarnate, the "Greatest God." Into his human image, the other gods were gradually transformed from their primitive animal shape, etc. The idea of anthropomorphic figures entered into Egyptian religion during the early historic period when gods were given human bodies.

Much of what is known of the general religious beliefs of ancient Egypt comes to us from funerary texts found in the tombs. The complexity of these beliefs and the enormous number of gods is due not only to the addition of deities over thousands of years but also the unwillingness to discard outmoded or contradictory beliefs.

The small figures of pottery, ivory, etc. representing probably a mother- or fertility goddess, are also found on much of the predynastic pottery. The predynastic cosmetic palettes shaped as animals, birds, fishes, etc. as well as small animal figures from tombs of the era were, most likely, representations of gods. During the Late Period, the cult of gods in animal- and other forms experienced a dramatic revival. The large animal cemeteries found in the cult centres confirm the popularity of this worship.

Polytheism, with its multiplicity of religious approaches to reality and to the some 700 different gods, lasted throughout Egyptian history excepting the short-lived introduction of the Aten sun-disk as the sole god, during and beginning somewhat before, the Amarna Period of the New Kingdom.

A distinction existed between official and private religion. The majority of religious texts allow an insight into official and funerary religion only. Texts and hymns glorifying the principal deities are extant as well as some practical compositions

28) LIST OF MAJOR GODS AND THEIR MOST USUAL ATTRIBUTES

relating to religious beliefs. Knowledge of private religious customs are scanty in comparison to the official versions. The great temples were built for the priests' practise of the various cults, carried out to preserve the cosmic order, and not for public worship. Except at the occasional state festivals when the general population participated in ceremonial processions, re-enactment of rituals, ordinary people had no part in state-cults.

During the New Kingdom, for almost four generations, workers of the Theban necropolis, many of them foreigners, lived at Deir-el-Medina. It is from this village that proof of an ancestor-cult in the Theban area came, with busts kept in niches and apparently worshipped (22).

Magical practises were the main ingredient of the religion of the common people. However, a complete description of these customs of the masses has never been found. Replicas of magical objects were manufactured en masse for the living and as part of mummy outfits. Amulets in the image of deities and sacred animals were worn and also scarabs, inscribed with expressions of religious beliefs, prayers and declarations of faith in one or the other deity, to protect the owner from dangers of any sort. Lists of lucky and unlucky days were consulted earnestly. Texts of an amuletic-protective nature and magical compositions for a great variety of purposes were written.

At the end of the New Kingdom children were made to wear small papyrus-roll amulets with texts which promised divine protection against many possible misfortunes.

AMULETS

All early, and some not so early, peoples have been shown to have believed, in varying degrees, in the power of magic. As a sociological pattern, this is, therefore, not a surprising fact to have been also part of Egyptian everyday life. By producing the image of a god, a person, an animal or inanimate object, one had not only created a species but also gained control over it, and achieved implicit confidence in the capacity of the particular image to do that, or protect from that, for which it stood. Magical rites and formulae were a prerequisite for effectiveness in this process.

22) DOMESTIC CULT SCULPTURE OF LIMESTONE
The bust is that of a woman in the conventional form characteristic of the New Kingdom. From other finds of this type from the Theban Necropolis workers' village (Deir el-Medina) the function of these representations of deceased family members was to be put into a niche of the dwelling as "household gods." Their great importance lies in the fact that there is so little material evidence of domestic art of ancient Egypt.

The specific reason for carving the figure in this shape is unknown. Some of the original gaudy colour is still visible on the piece (wig: blue, modius: bright red, flesh: yellow). The ears, as seen so often in Egyptian art, are overly large, with pierced lobes for earrings. The ousekh or multi-registered necklace of polychrome glass, of metal or of inlays is partially covered by unusually thick lappets of the wig.

A slightly stern, very individualised expression of the face is accompanied by a feature of the earlier part of Dynasty XIX in the rendering of the (originally black painted) eyes: the flat diagonal plane arrangement, creating a somewhat sleepy effect.

Magical practices were mainly designed as a defense against negative forces. Where particular images were feared because they might turn into life-versions of their threatening representations on hieroglyphs they were mutilated into harmless shapes or pierced with arrows or, similar to the African nail fetishes still in use, made to resemble pin-cushions full of bristling knives.

Magical "healing statues" inscribed with magical texts against all sorts of physical danger also had their place. In order to be assured that existing wounds would heal and no further harm occur, one had to pour water over such figures and then drink the water. Such figures were, particularly in the Late Period, set up in a place accessible to all. Magical spells accompanied prescriptions for illnesses, in hopes of either increasing the efficacy of the prescription or of replacing it with the spells.

Amulets were produced in an infinite variety, and were made of metal, ivory, precious stones or most commonly of steatite (often glazed) or faience. Sizes varied enormously, the smallest amulets being approx. 1/3". Some of the more commonly produced amulets for the living were:

ANKH sign of immortality, representing life and afterlife, shaped as a cross with a loop as the upper vertical member.

DJED pillar, column, or tree shaped symbol of stability and endurance.

SEMA, a stylized lung and windpipe, symbol of Union.

SA, looking like a rolled-up papyrus stem, believed to be a general defense against any hostile force of domestic nature, thus often shown as attribute of Thoeris (Tau-eret) and Bes.

TYET, knot or girdle of Isis, symbolic of welfare.

PHALLIC symbols as protection against impotence.

KHEPER (Khepri), the scarabeus sacer, as symbol of resurrection and rising sun, the most important and frequently applied amuletic device.

Amultes of royal emblems included the various crowns, the vulture and cobra; all of these were thought to give the wearer kingly powers.

Anthropomorphic figures and sacred animals such as the cat, frog, lion, and hare, were part of a long list of creatures fashioned into amuletic jewellery for the living. The following were particularly popular for their presumed magic properties: Isis in several arrangements of attributes, Anubis, Thoeris, Bes, the composite deity Ptah-Sokar-Osiris, and many more.

Amulets were an important part of the funerary supply, inserted in the mummy wrappings, placed over the limb or organ for which each amulet had an especial protective power. Formulae for the arrangement of amulets on mummies were given in the "Book of the Dead" and the "Ritual of Embalmment." The most commonly used amulets on mummies were:

HEART-SCARAB, a scarab usually of faience with wings attached to the body of the beetle, and placed over the heart. The flat underside was inscribed with a plea to the heart not to act as unfavourable witness in the forthcoming judgement in the presence of Osiris.

UDJAT-EYE, placed onto several parts of the body, in particular over the abdominal incision as a powerful protection, sometimes made of gold; also on the eye, neck, below the heart, below the right knee, above the foot area. In funerary use, the Udjat-eye represented resurrection. There were also double udjat-eyes and sometimes an amulet consisting of more than two of this symbol.

DJEBAUI, symbolising two fingers of Horus and Seth as they assisted Osiris on his ascension to heaven.

MENYET, shaped like a bead necklace, associated with Hathor, representing physical well-being and pleasure (29).

SECHEM, a papyrus sceptre as representation of physical vigour.

PESESH-KEF, a miniature version of the implement used in the "Opening of the Mouth Ceremony" to animate the mummy, shaped like a forked flint knife.

WRS, a sign like a headrest, an important amulet as it protected against the mummy's decapitation by grave robbers or in the Netherworld.

Magico-religious spells were inscribed onto royal pyramid chambers of Dynasties V and VI, called "Pyramid Texts." Later usurped for similar purposes in the burials of, first, local princes and then high officials, they gradually deteriorated from the original form to become eventually the "Coffin Texts" of religious writings.

A Middle Kingdom peculiar type of burial amulet was the miniature figure of a hippopotamus, possibly believed to protect the tomb or assist the dead in his rebirth as a living spirit. Also from Middle Kingdom graves came magical wands, used by the living as well. Made of hippopotamus ivory, they were engraved either with the image of domestic deities or beings against whom the wands were believed to give protection. From New Kingdom times onwards, ordinary small scarabs, inscribed with divine symbols and magical texts, were added to the amuletic equipment of the mummy.

During the New Kingdom, particularly its later phase, as well as the Late Period, as a special funerary feature, ivory wands and hypocephali were included in burials along with amulets. The hypocephali were placed beneath the head of the mummy. They were usually of linen, stiffened with plaster and decorated with vignettes of various deities and extracts from the "Book of the Dead" which were designed to bring warmth to the body. The hypocephali represented the pupil and iris of the eye of Horus/Ra/Shu. Deities represented on these, to whom great power was attributed, were the four sons of Horus, Hathor, the WAS sceptre carried by a Janus-headed god, three divine boats, etc. Sometimes, the hypocephali were made of papyrus, rarely of bronze.

30) AMULETS
BES — FIGURE

No suspension hole—dark green faience—richly plumed headdress, one of his characteristic features. Bes is represented as a dwarf-deity with leonine features, wearing a leopard skin and pendant with the head of the animal; protruding tongue. He is often shown resting his hand upon the SA symbol of protection against hostile forces. His hands rest on his abdomen symbolic of his protective powers for women in child-birth. Bes was of foreign origin, possibly introduced into the Egyptian pantheon from the Sudan. His ancestor might also have been Khumbaba of Mesopotamian legend. In reliefs, Bes is shown frontally in contrast to the conventional profile rendering of Egyptian portraiture. He is a widely represented domestic god; as helper of women in child-birth his image was put in the mammisi, the birth houses in the temple where the ritual rebirth of the god was annually enacted. He was the buffoon god and marriage god; he presided over the toilet of ladies and thus is often shown on handles of mirrors and other toilet articles such as rouge boxes, scent bottles, etc., also on headrests, for he was believed to "send sweet dreams." He was thought to protect against snakes and an assortment of other dangers, and represented on amuletic wands of ivory which seem to have been used to mark time in dancing. Wands of ivory were sometimes shaped as hands. His image was often found in middle-class houses of the Late Period, and children were named after him.

ISIS SUCKLING THE INFANT HORUS

Upper part only extant—Nile-green glazed terracotta—throne ideogramme—Buto cobra on forehead—suspension hole on plinth at back.

Horus specifically as the son of Isis, Hariesis. Isis = Greek form of Aset or Eset, member of the Divine Ennead of Heliopolis, daughter of Geb and Nut, wife and sister of Osiris, sister also of Selkit, Seth and Nephthys. With Selkit, Neith and Nephthys she was one of the four protector goddesses guarding coffins and canopic jars. Isis and Nephthys mourned the dead Osiris as the "Great and the Little Kite," fluttering with lamentations over his body. By extension, the two goddesses became the divine mourners for all dead. In the Osirian legand, according to Plutarch, Isis reassembled the pieces of her murdered husband with the help of Nephthys, to become the mother of Horus, and the divine mother. This offspring of Osiris and son of Isis = Hor-sa-eset was in his youth called "infant Horus" = Hor-pa-khrad, or, by the Greeks, Harpokrates. The traditional attributes of childhood were the sidelock and forefinger placed on the mouth. This latter fact was mistakenly thought to imply silence and as a result the Greeks considered the young god as divinity of discretion.

As the suckler of kings Isis is shown with a throne-shaped ideogramme atop her head, her name meaning "seat" and possibly pointing to her origin as a goddess of the royal throne of Lower Egypt. Her first known place of worship as a protective deity was near Bubastis but her exact origin is unknown. As fertility goddess and eternal mother she bears similarity to the Sumerian goddess of the planet Venus, Astarte. With her tears shed over her dead husband, Isis was thought to have caused the first inundation of the Nile; thus she represents the fertile part of Egypt. In the later period, she is often represented with a lunar disk within lyriform or cow's horns, referring to her identification with Hathor.

During the Late Period, particularly in Ptolemaic times, the cult of Isis spread all over and beyond the Mediterranean world. Her principal cult centre was at Philae where the sanctuary remained open to her cult until the sixth century A. D. The Greeks associated Isis with Demeter and Aphrodite. Greek settlers in Egypt considered Isis and Harpokrates as healers and saviours. During the Roman Empire, nine important temples were built for her worship in Rome alone.

THOERIS

Thoueris — Tau-erat — Taweret — Apet — Opet — "the Great" — on pedestal — limestone with light green, dulled glazing — legs are re-glued — glaze missing from right breast and left nostril — suspension hole below mane and above tail — represented as a female hippopotamus with pendant mammae, standing on hind legs — usually she holds the hieroglyphic sign SA for protection, made into a plait of rolled papyrus — she fulfilled the same function as Bes for women in childbirth — as a very popular beneficient deity she was particularly worshipped at Thebes. The possibility of the small hippopotamus figurines and hippopotamus-shaped palettes of predynastic times being the forerunner of Thoeris is still disputed among authorities. Thoeris was, all throughout Egyptian history, and by all levels of society, much revered (31).

ANUBIS

Anpu — terracotta with light green glazing — broken off obliquely below the knee area, otherwise in superb condition except for missing tip of nose — suspension hole on plinth at back below mane — brilliant glazing. Anubis is shown in anthropomorphic form with what is referred to as jackal head, although strictly speaking, the real jackal is not evident in Egypt, while the common roving dog resembling the wolf is taken for a model of Anubis' head.

Anubis had accompanied Osiris on the latter's conquest of the world and on the murder of "The Good One" he originated embalming by embalming Osiris. Prior to Osiris' ascendancy to prominence, Anubis = "Lord of the Land" was the great funerary god with many sanctuaries built for him. He was the great necropolis god, the god of embalmers who donned masks in his likeness on carrying out their work. Anubis led the deceased to Amenti, the region of the dead where the souls were judged. He held and watched the scales in the "Weighing of the Heart in the Hall of Judgment." In Greek usage, he was given the accoutrements of Hermes along with the familiar jackal head, and called Hermanubis. When represented as a jackal (XIX), his image was coated in black resin in reference to the sacred gum used in the embalming, the colour of which also represents resurrection. In this he resembled the actual, very black dogs on which his image was based.

A god of remote times names Imiut, meaning "He who is in his wrappings" was eventually identified with Anubis. A fetish belonging to this ancient god, shaped as a pole terminating in a lotus bud, from which hung an inflated animal skin with a tail of copper wire ending in a papyrus flower, is ocasionally represented as an attribute of Anubis.

BES

Double figure of openwork carving — bone — head missing — Broad Collar necklace — large navel area — bandy-legged, hands holding sides of prominent abdomen — superbly carved.

Low relief carving of side shows an image of Isis, with Nephthys on the other side.

Low relief carving on base, broken in several places — hieroglyphs of scarab, cat, Udjat eye.

All: C.

BULLFROG

Emblematic of Heqet (Hqt), goddess of Antinopolis, frog-goddess and symbol of dampness of primeval waters — wife of Khnum — talisman; no suspension holes — Nephrite — modern word for frog/toad = Pageget, the ancient Egyptian Q(e)r(e)r.

OTHER PRINCIPAL GODS AND DEITIES AND THEIR IN-
CARNATION ANIMALS:
AMON, AMEN, AMUN
    One of the chief gods of Thebes, of uncertain origin,
represented as a man, sometimes ithyphallic, united with the sun-
god—husband of Mut, father of Khonsu—ram with curved
horns, or goose.
ATEN
    God of the sun disk, worshipped as the sole creator god
by Akhenaten.
BASTET
    Sometimes MUT, cat goddess of Babastis, beneficient
deity of the Late Period.
BUTO, EDJO, WADJET
    Cobra-goddess of Buto, deity of Lower Egypt, worn on
the royal diadem, personal protector goddess of the king.
HAPY
    God of inundation of the Nile—represented as a man
with heavy breasts and zigzag design of water over his body.
HORUS
    The sun god from the Late Predynastic Period—identi-
fied with the king—falcon deity in anthropomorphic form—he
appeared in a multitude of shapes and corresponding names—
main centres of worship were at Behedet in the Delta and at Edfu
and Hierankopolis in Upper Egypt—avenger of his father Osiris.
MA'AT
    Goddess of truth, right, orderly conduct, represented as
a woman with an ostrich feather atop her head which is her symbol—during the Amarna period of the Aten cult much emphasis
was put on the incorporation of this principle, as MAAT meant
in full "Order and Reality," the fundamental element of the
monotheistic faith with its simplicity and directness.
NEITH
    Goddess of Sais, wearing the Red Crown—according to
Saite legend, Neith took credit for creating the world by utter-
ance—identified by the Greeks with Athena—one of the four
protector goddesses guarding coffins and canopic jars along with
Isis, Nephthys and Selkit; in particular she guarded the stomach—emblem: shield with crossed arrows.
NEPHTHYS
    Daughter of Geb and Nut, sister of Isis, Osiris, and
Seth; she mourned with Isis as the "Little Kite" and became one
of the two "Divine Mourners"—as guardian of the canopic jar
she was in charge of the lungs—her emblem looks like a small
pillar with a crescent moon atop.
NU
    God of the primeval chaos.
NUTH
    Goddess of heavens, wife of Geb, member of the ori-
ginal ennead—represented as a woman whose nude body forms
the arch of heaven.

OSIRIS-ASAR

God of the underworld, identified as dead king, god of inundation and vegetation, son of Geb and Nuth, god of the underworld and judge of the dead—up to Late Old Kingdom times the king considered posthumously Osiris, after that this applied to all dead—as Osiris-Apis identified with the sacred bull of Serapis—anthropomorphic, mummified.

PTAH

Creator god and chief deity of the Memphite triad, husband of Sekhmet and father of Nefertum—he was the embodiment of the sacred bull—when Memphis became the capital city of the kings of Egypt, Ptah was shown as the creator god, and a new creation legend was coined for this = Het-ka-ptah "The House of Ptah"—represented as a man, mummiform, possibly originally as a statue (14)—patron god of craftsmen, he had created the world on a potter's wheel—equated by the Greeks with Hephaestus—as PTAH-SEKER-OSIRIS he was the synthesis of the gods of creation, death and the Netherworld.

RA-RE

Sun god, head of the great ennead, supreme judge, represented as falcon-headed.

RE-HARAKHTY

God as a falcon with characteristics of RE and Horus = "Horus of the Horizon."

SEKHMET

Consort of Ptah and mother of Nefertum, member of the Memphite triad—lion-headed, she brought destruction to Re's enemies—goddess of war, battle, vengeance, epidemics, doctors.

SELKIT

One of the four protector goddesses, she guarded the canopic jar containing the intestines—identified with the scorching heat of the sun, her emblem is the scorpion.

SETH

God of darkness and destruction, storms and violence—brother and murderer of Osiris, rival of Horus—brother and husband of Nephthys, father of Anubis—identified with a multitude of animals: pig, ass, okapi, hippopotamus but represented as animal of unidentified type—equated with Typhon by the Greeks.

SOBEK-SEBEK-SUCHOS

Crocodile-god worshipped throughout Egypt but primarily in the Fayum, at Gebelein and Kom Ombo in Upper Egypt—represented as a crocodile or anthropomorphic with a crocodile head—Sebek had partaken in the murder of Osiris and was punished by being changed into a crocodile—he caught the four sons of Horus out of the water with a net.

UNNEFER-WENEN-NEFER-ONNOPHRIS

Name given to Osiris after his resurrection, meaning "He who is continually happy."

32) JANUS-HEADED HATHOR

Broken off at neck — cow-ears — limestone with traces of light green glazing — superbly modelled features (C. 613).

Hathor, or Athyr, was the most ancient and complex deity of Egypt, and her functions, attributes and places of worship are numerous. On the palette of King Nar-mer, her cow-head appears four times, representing the corners of the world. She is shown either as a cow-headed woman, or with the sun-disk surmounting her head, within cow horns, or as the "celestial cow" symbolising the divine nourishment. She was often represented as the "Lady of the Sycamore," hiding in her shape as a cow in the foliage, appearing with bread and water of welcome for the deceased. In the Theban and Memphite necropolis areas, she was made the guardian of the mountain of the dead and called "Queen of the West." Hathor was the only deity whose head alone is sometimes shown as capital on a particular type of column, called the Hathor column. It represented the sistrum, the musical instrument sacred to Hathor as goddess of love, dance and music. The sistrum as the fetish of Hathor was thought to drive away evil spirits. Handles of sistra were often decorated with the image of Hathor's head. As protectress of women she also presided over their toilet, thus her likeness appeared on handles of mirrors and other toilet articles. The "Seven Hathors," much like our fairies in function, decided the fate of a newly born child. The Sinai "mistress of the land of Mefket," Hathor was worshipped in Phoenicia as "The Lady of Byblos." She was the goddess of gold, hence of Punt, the source of much gold used in Egypt.

Originally a sky-goddess, she was also represented as the daughter of Ra, and wife as well as sometimes mother of Horus. As the suckler of kings, she was in the Late Period identified with Isis. The Greeks associated her with Aphrodite.

31) PANEL FROM ARM OF CHAIR OF PRINCESS SIT-AMUN, "BELOVED ELDEST DAUGHTER OF THE KING"

The first truly royal chair ever discovered from ancient Egypt, it belonged to Akhenaten's daughter. The panel has two figures of Bes, the benevolent domestic deity, one brandishing two knives to drive away evil beings, the other holding a tambourine. Tail, mane and ears of a lion, he is shown in part-human form as the protective household god in general. Between the two stands the female pregnant hippopotamus goddess Thoeris, Patroness of women in childbirth. The figures were carved separately from the chair and tenoned onto the panel, worked as bas relief and gilded.

While Thoeris was an ancient deity of Egypt, the "imported" demi-god Bes gained in favour not before the New Kingdom as a household god.

MUMMIFICATION

Faint echoes of a belief in after-life, evidenced in grave-finds from prehistoric times, can be established in later dynastic Egyptian religion regarding funerary and mummification customs. Mummification was regarded as an imitation of the very first embalming, that of Osiris by Anubis, the originator of this funerary ritual. The hope for resurrection, the continuation of life after the physical death of a person, was to be effected by the complicated process of embalming, coupled with strictly pre-scribed recitations of magical texts by attendant lecture-priests (Kher-heb), each text corresponding to the various stages of mummification.

After the body had been prepared for the placement into the coffin, the ceremony of the "Opening of the Mouth" or replacement of the soul which had fled the person's body at the moment of death took place. Its intent was to restore all the faculties to the deceased with which he could enjoy life in the hereafter. The implement used in this ceremony was called Urt-hekau, "Great Magician." In keeping with the belief that the deceased would experience a new existence in his tomb, the same needs that he required on earth had to be satisfied in terms of food, clothing, funerary furniture, etc. In the course of the vary-ing funerary customs, these items were placed in the tomb (either in actual form, or models, or else as tomb paintings) together with records of the deceased's lifetime activities, contemporary historic episodes or religious ceremonies.

Following a death, women mourners rushed into the street uttering loud lamentations and, in the traditional gesture of mourning, raised their arms above their heads, defiling their heads with mud and dust, and renting their clothes. No perman-ent building for embalming existed; the Per-nefer or structure for the purpose was dismantled after use. The degree of elaboration of a funeral could be pre-selected from models of mummies and mummy cases and displays of funerary furniture. A choice could also be made for inner and outer coffins, canopic jars, ushabtis and, from the New Kingdom, excerpts of copies from the "Book of the Dead." The ancient Egyptian title of this religious com-position was "The Chapter of coming forth by Day," i.e., a knowledge of the book would enable the deceased to obtain immediate immortality.

The viscera was removed by a "cutter" via an incision in the left flank, the area first marked by a scribe, from as early as Dynasty IV onwards. The body cavity was packed and the body placed into a natron solution or dry natron for seventy days. The brain (from Middle Kingdom times) was also removed, at least by Dynasty XVIII via the nostril. In the periods of careful mummification, subcutaneous packing was done, as well as artificial eyes placed over the shrunken orbits, to give the body as life-like an appearance as possible. Then, supplied with a multitude of amulets over the appropriate parts of the body, bandaging (each digit and limb separately) took place. As in painting, so a distinction was made between the sexes in the bandages: darker colouration for men than for women.

All material that had come in contact with the mummy during the embalming process was carefully gathered and stuffed into large pots and buried near the tomb of the dead person. It was believed that even as much as a hair of the dead seen by an enemy might endow the latter with a power to bewitch the dead.

While the essential belief in the existence of after-life remained constant throughout ancient Egypt, customs of burial over the millenia changed. Only seven mummies from the Old Kingdom are definitely known because the embalming method was not as yet well developed.

In general during New Kingdom times, mummification was done very carefully. It reached its peak in the succeeding Dynasty XXI during the parallel reigns of the kings at Tanis and the priest-kings at Thebes, reflecting the conservation attitude of the latter as further evidenced in the salvage work done on the royal tombs pillaged during the preceding era. Inscriptions on mummy wrappings record efforts by priests of Dynasty XXI to hide mummies, etc.

Less and less care was taken in mummification during Ptolemaic times in the treatment of the body. Binding and appearance of the actual mummy case were considered more important. (XX).

In the Roman Period bandages were often arranged in an elaborate geometric pattern, with an encaustic wax panel inserted in the bandages covering the head (XXI).

In the 19th century A. D. with great interest generated in Egyptian antiquities generally and the discovery of mummies in particular, a veritable "industry" by the fellahins sprang up. Concoctions of wire, birds and animals of all sorts were mummified, buried and ultimately "discovered" for the purpose. Celebrated among these is the case in which Ma-ka-Re, High Priestess of Amun, probably a half-sister of the wife of the last king of Dynasty XXI, was ostensibly buried with her female child who died in infancy. The latter turned out under X-ray examination (1968) to be the mummy of a female hamadryas baboon. Possibly, this was legitimately done in order to bury a substitute child with the mother who predeceased her baby daughter.

CANOPIC JARS

The oldest known vessel made to hold the embalmed viscera of the deceased, removed from the body in the mummification process, dates from Dynasty VI. They were made of pottery or stone, often limestone or alabaster, with a lid on top. The earliest types had ordinary lids; from the end of the Old Kingdom onwards until the end of Dynasty XVIII they were made in the shape of a human head (XXII). After that the jar-stoppers were carved in the form of appropriate minor deities, the four sons of Horus who had guardianship over the stomach, intestines, lungs and liver (XXIIa). For the respective organs, the lids represented: Duamutef (jackal-headed: stomach); Qebsenuf (falcon-headed: intestines); Hapy, (ape-headed: lungs); Imsety, (human-headed: liver).

Each jar was identified with one of four protective female deities: stomach with Neith, intestines with Selkit, lungs with Nephthys, and liver with Isis.

Chests to contain the jars were made of alabaster or wood, sometimes gilded. These were placed near the mummy so as to unite symbolically the jars with the body after the appropriate spells and rituals had been performed.

Mummification practices changed often during the whole period of Egyptian antiquity. It became the custom during Dynasty XXI to place the four organs, made up into separate packages, inside the body cavity, each accompanied by a wax figure of the respective son of Horus. But even then a set of canopic jars was included in the tomb so as to adhere to religious formalities. Similar dummy jars were used during Ptolemaic times, when the viscera were often left in the body.

The term canopic is, strictly speaking, a misnomer. It refers to the legendary Greek hero Canopus, the pilot of Sparta's king Menelaus. Having died en route home from Troy, he was buried at Canopus in Egypt and locally worshipped in the form of a human-headed jar with a swollen body, the latter giving the shape to all such jars, with minor modification towards a less rounded form in some.

SHABTIS—USHABTIS

The shabti figure was a specialised form of the earlier servant figures in Old Kingdom tombs. With the triumph of the Osirian faith, which was less materialistic in concept than the older belief of the sun-cult of Ra, it seemed less important to supply the deceased with models of people performing a number of services they carried out for him in life.

From earliest times, the corvee had existed in Egypt, whereby labourers were drafted en masse for public works during the annual inundation of the country by the Nile. It was believed that similar duties would have to be performed in the Osirian realm. The shabti figures were provided to exempt the deceased, including royal personages, from such labour. They were considered deputies for the dead.

The earliest known formula to invoke the shabti to perform duties on behalf of its owner, from a wooden coffin of the Middle Kingdom, reads in part . . ."Behold me, thou shalt say to any messenger come for me . . . take up your mattocks, hoes, yokes and baskets in your hands, as any man does for his master."

The etymology of the earlier name shabti for these figures seems to have been doubtful to the Egyptian themselves. As some were made of wood from the persea or shawab tree, this may have been the origin of the term. From the New Kingdom onwards, they were called ushabti, lit. "answerer."

Many royal shabtis were found, some of them of elaborate workmanship. Most, but not all, carry the royal crock and flail, some an ankh sign in each hand (XXIV). Shabtis for royalty were made in temple-workshops directed by a priest called "Chief fashioner of amulets" (since the principal production of the shops was that of amulets inserted into mummy wrappings). Shabtis were mummiform figures; they were not formal representations of the deceased.

The first examples, fashioned of wax, were found in tombs from Dynasty XI. From the end of the Middle Kingdom onwards, they were made of wood, alabaster, white or yellow limestone, sandstone, quartzite of several shades, granite, sometimes bronze, but, most frequently from Dynasty XVIII on, of faience and glazed stones.

The earliest shabtis were simply inscribed with the name of the deceased. New Kingdom shabtis bore inscriptions of the shabti-text, a chapter from the "Book of the Dead." At this time, shabtis were first made with agricultural tools in their hands — hoes, mattocks and baskets. Throughout the later part of the New Kingdom and the Late Period, during which green faience was primarily used for their making (XXV), the design of shabtis deteriorated. Finely modelled pieces were again made in Dynasty XXV times. The use of shabtis seems to have been discontinued at the end of the Dynastic Period.

Placed singly into burials, the earliest made shabtis were true deputies of the deceased. Later, particularly in royal tombs, large numbers of them were buried, with the greatest increase from Dynasty XVIII. Some New Kingdom shabtis, buried singly, within a separate small coffin, may have had some other than a deputising function. Generally, however, during late New Kingdom times, it was customary to provide one shabti for each day of the year, organized into "work-gangs" of ten each, with an overseer to each group, so that the total was 401. The overseer figures were not, usually, supplied with agricultural tools and represented in mummiform, but rather wore a kilt and carried a whip of office. The greatest number of shabtis (approx. 700) was found in the tomb of Sethi I, the first important king of Dynasty XIX. Shabti-boxes accomodated these large numbers and boards bearing decrees concerning the deceased's habits were added.

Because of the long tradition of their use and relative low cost of production, shabtis are among the most common objects preserved from Egyptian antiquity (38).

38) USHABTI
 Of faience and badly damaged, this nevertheless retains some of the striking modelling of the facial details, while the Osirid body was given rather rudimentary treatment. C. 617

SEALS AND SCARABS

During the so-called Jemdet Nasr Period, that is the time immediately preceding the foundation of Dynasty I, Egypt adopted the Mesopotamian cylinder seal bearing an intaglio design which could be transferred to soft clay. The usual purpose of these seals was to mark ownership or authenticity or as funerary objects bearing the name of the deceased (33). The earliest extant is that of King Nar-mer (Menes) of Dynasty I. They were in use for royalty as late as the reign of Ramesses II and after that for private personages only until Dynasty XXVI. However, later specimens of these are extremely rare. Cylinder seals found were of copper and bronze, but the bulk was of black or white steatite with green or blue glazing. Ivory, green jasper, haematite and particularly wood, was used for the production of these. Many clay impressions made from cylinder seals were also excavated.

During the Asiatic invasion of the Delta at the end of the Old Kingdom perforated hemispherical seals appeared, so-called button seals. In the Middle Kingdom these developed into the characteristic Egyptian scarab, with an enormous diffusion over all of the Near Eastern areas for many centuries to come. The Hyksos in particular took up the production of scarabs with great enthusiasm and in great numbers.

Much like the cylinder or stamp seals, the scarabs were used to stamp clay sealings and were often mounted on rings or provided with holes for suspension. They were also worn as amuletic devices. The stomach or flat side of the scarab was inscribed with either the name and title of the owner, dedicatory texts or royal names because of the presumed protective qualities of the latter. Design and inscription varied according to the purpose of the respective scarab; some are merely decorative without any narrative significance. In the same way as our commemorative medals, historical scarabs were issued, with the name of the king and a narrative recording the event. Amenophis III issued a large scarab commemorating the construction of a pleasure lake for his royal wife Tiye, as well as a number of lion-hunt scarabs and marriage scarabs. The importance of scarabs in general to archaeology is invaluable; the social, religious, and cultural history of Egypt could be learnt from these objects alone. Scarabs varied in size from approximately 1 cm. to 10 cm. They were made of a variety of materials including limestone, faience and a number of semi-precious stones, but the majority of them seem to have been made of steatite and glazed. In this latter medium scarabs were made throughout the Dynastic Period. Steatite, being a soft stone, is particularly well suited for carving small objects and provides an ideal base for glazing, as it does not disintegrate under heat.

33) CYLINDER SEAL, BORED; BLACK STEATITE*—AND IMPRESSION

The panther-like animal, supplied with a vertical bar, occurs on other cylinder seals from the period. The inscription reads "belonging to Tehuti, Tekhi, a private person." The short, thick form of this cylinder seal is near-identical with early Chaldean and Elamite examples. This type was found associated with larger ones in tombs of Dynasty I. It disappeared approximately at the date of the third king of that dynasty, to be succeeded in general use until Dynasty VI by a long and relatively thin type. C.

*Published: Alan Rowe, "Egyptian Scarabs," 1936, S1.

Scarabs were shaped "naturalistically" to simple scaraboid form. On some the prothorax and elytra were clearly marked, on many others not indicated. Some scarabs have a ram's head. The backs of scarabs were sometimes inlaid with stone or pigment, as was also occasionally done with the hieroglyphs on the flat side.

The heart-scarab was the most important amuletic accessory placed within the mummy wrappings.

Scarab, the SCARABEUS SACER, representing the god KHEPRI (Kheper) as the sun on his appearance every morning was identified with the creator-god RA, and represented as a beetle within, or holding, the sun-disk. The Egyptian word Kheper is the same for the sun-god, the scarab itself and existence; the scarab served as the hieroglyphic sign for all three. The Egyptians had associated the beetle's rolling a ball of dung and its young coming out of the ball (actually: pear-shaped) with the invisible power rolling the sun across the sky.

The black or anthracite-coloured beetle was seldom shown in this colour because of the difficulty of obtaining obsidian and the lack of any native stones approximating it.

In ancient Egyptian medicine the beetle was employed externally. Wings and body were made into an ointment for stiff joints; the elytra into a salve to help in childbirth. In order to render certain spells ineffective, a large beetle, head and wings removed, was burned, put in fat and applied. To drug an enemy, beetles were burnt in a gum and then mixed into a drink.

Scarabs were collected and traded throughout the Mediterranean from antiquity, even though the specimens often were of poor quality. Since they continue to be the most popular objects from ancient Egypt, and despite the many thousands that were found in cemeteries and KOMS (Fellahin equivalent of the Arabic "tell") the manufacture of forgeries continues (XXII, 34-37).

34) SILVER-LEAD ALLOY STAMP SEAL

Oblong, flat, two-sided. Cartouche: R-mn-hpr (Ra-men-kheper, transliterated into "May Ra continue to bring into existence") — Tuthmosis III, Dynasty XVIII — sphinx couchant, wearing a Broad Collar necklace, ceremonial beard and wig — above her back is an uraeus — reverse: KA sign, uraeus with Pshent bi-laterally — (C. 194)

OVOID SCARAB

Green schist — cartouche bears three royal names making it suspect as to authenticity: Men-kheper-Ra: "existence, being of Ra is firm"; Kheper-ka-Ra: "becoming of Ra"; Setep-en-Ra: "Chosen of Ra." (C. 356)

35)   THREE SCARABS
    1) Steatite. Head of falcon with Ibes crown: possibly the bird of Menthu, god of Hermontis, war-god of the king; uraeus' body to sides of crown — cartouche: Men-kheper-Ra (C. 263)
    2) King's foot steps on serpent erect — king brandishes spear shown behind his head, quiver placed behind (i. e. next to) him; ankh sign (C. 287B)
    3) Ankh sign flanked by two falcons and two uraei erect, all surmounted by sun-disk; falcons placed on NEW = "all" sign — glazed (C. 203)

36) THREE SCARABS — STEATITE
    1) Within intact gold mount — side panels: uraei supporting White Crown, KA sign above — centre: ankh signs, two figures of Ma'at, two DJED pillars, NUB sign below = gold (C. 202)
    2) Hyksos, probably Dynasties XV–XVII, centre: ankh, EIN and RA, annule border design, deeply incised. Hyksos style scarabs continued to be made until the beginning of Dynasty XVIII. From former Hyksos sites in Palestine a great number of them were found. (C. 252)
    3) Well engraved, Kheper between two Djed pillars, NUB sign = gold above, KA upper centre, flanked by NEFER signs and NEB sign above (C. 299)

37)   THREE SCARABS
    1) Top scarab type — splay legs of exaggerated size — eleytra and prothorax on scarab incised — striation design radiating from it — steatite with remnants of yellow glazing — cartouche on base: Men-kheper-Ra—Amenophis III, Dynasty XVIII (C. 226)
    2) Alabaster — fairly defaced, design: king wearing White Crown, in offertory gesture towards ankh sign — cartouche behind him and SHEN sign for eternity above (C. 225)
    3) Steatite — cartouche: KA sign — Hotep above — continuous rope design border — Hyksos, Dynasty XII (C. 360)

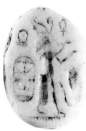

BUILDING MATERIALS

I) Brick: sun-baked Nile mud bricks were used in Egypt for domestic buildings, as well as some official structures and, continuing after the New Kingdom, temples to local gods. Wooden tomb models and tomb paintings show the method of brickmaking.

Post-inundation alluvium of specified consistency was taken in baskets or jars to the brickyard, to be mixed with water with the help of the foot or a hoe. To improve the adhesive quality, as well as the strength of the mud, chopped straw was kneaded into it. In baskets this mixture was then taken to the actual brickmaker, who used a hollow, rectangular wooden mould of a specific size for the production, after which the mass was left to dry for two to three days in the fierce heat.

Kilns for brick-making, although evident by about 600 B. C. during the reign of King Necho II of the Saite Period, were not generally used until Roman times. Even now, in Egyptian villages, bricks are most commonly made by the ancient sun-dried method.

Occasionally, bricks would receive a stamp with the name of the reigning king or a high official. It is, in some cases, possible to date the erection of a building by the size of bricks used. This varied according to the final purpose of the brick. For house construction, the brick-size was approx. 9 X 6 X 3," for walls of towns, temples and fortresses approx. 12 X 6 X 3" in the Middle Kingdom to approx. 16 X 8 X 6" in the New Kingdom.

The architectural term adobe used in Latin American and Mediterranean lands is derived from the ancient Egyptian word TOBE for brick.

A type of brick was used as amuletic protection in the New Kingdom and later. It consisted of a set of four magical bricks, put into wall-niches of the burial chamber. Representing the four directions, they each had impressed into them an amuletic symbol: the northern, a mummified human figure of wood; southern, a reed fitted with a wick (torch); eastern, a jackal of unbaked clay; and the western, a blue glaze- composition Djed pillar. Made of unbaked clay, the bricks were inscribed with individual texts from the "Book of the Dead." They were thought to prevent the approach of enemies of the deceased from the four cardinal points.

II) Stones: building in stone began during Dynasty I, experiencing a rapid development after the construction of the first great all-stone monumental building, the Step Pryamid of King Djoser of Dynasty III. In the subsequent reign, and thereafter, large limestone blocks were used for the building of large funerary structures. The use of copper, and later, bronze tools enabled the quarrying and dressing of huge stone slabs.

The great durability of stone was a factor in its popularity for monuments, which were to last forever. Until New Kingdom times, local cult temples as well as, always, ordinary houses of all degrees of elaboration, continued to be constructed of mud-brick. For these, local limestone was incorporated into parts requiring stronger materials, such as lintels, doorposts, thresholds, column-bases and slabs for wash-rooms.

The three main building stones were limestone, sandstone and granite. Cliffs and hills edging the Nile Valley from Cairo to Edfu in Upper Egypt are mostly limestone, of varying quality. The best comes from Tura, south of Cairo, as well as from parts of the Theban Necropolis area. Fine white Tura limestone was used for the outer facing of the great pyramid of Cheops (Khufu). In Arabic times, this was stripped off and re-used, leaving only the very top part of it intact. Tura limestone was the ideal vehicle for the many delicate shallow relief carvings. It was highly prized in dynastic times. The man-made caves of the quarry, in which pillars were left standing to prevent the collapse of the roof, became a favourite tourist site in Greek and Roman times, described by Herodotus and Strabo.

Sandstone was the main building material employed in the reign of Tuthmosis III, and from then on became the favourite stone for the construction of the great temples of Upper Egypt, partly because of the proximity of the Gebel-el-Sisila quarries, in easy transport reach of Thebes. The most spectacular building made of this material is the temple at Abu Simbel, hewn out of sandstone cliffs to a distance of 180', with four colossal figures of Rameses II.

Quartzite, a very hard compact species of sandstone, used to a limited extent in building, was quarried from Gebel-el-Ahmar, northeast of Cairo.

Granite was used in the making of columns, doorways, shrines, and small burial chambers. Both the pink and black type came from the First Cataract region at Aswan, from at least as early as the Old Kingdom. A highly desireable stone, it was often imitated by painting limestone.

For embellishment of walls in the most important palace rooms, alabaster was used occasionally. The most highly valued type came from Hatnub, a desert site near Tell el-Amarna in Middle Egypt.

Basalt, of varying colour, was another stone sometimes employed in architecture, particularly for paving and lower courses.

STONEWORKING

In the early Predynastic Period, alabaster (calcite), basalt, brescia (red, green and white), granite of pink and grey variety, porphiritic rock and softer type of limestone were worked into vessels, the earliest of which were made of basalt. Additionally, in the later Predynastic Period, fine green schist, speckled diorite, serpentine and steatite were used for this purpose.

From Dynastic times, a great number of stone vessels were recovered from royal, as well as from private tombs. A hoard of several thousand was found in King Djoser's Step Pyramid. A vase of the last king of Dynasty II had a gold cover imitating a cloth atop the jar, tied with string.

A great variety of vessels required low stands; occasionally stand and vessel were made in one piece. In tomb paintings, many of these vessels are represented on their stands.

Complete mastery of the art of working often hard stone, shaping it as though it were clay is exemplified in thousands of objects (XVa).

From the Late Pre-Dynastic Period on, the making of stone vessels was greatly facilitated by the aid of the bow-drill. Representations in tomb scenes of vessel-making and unfinished specimens show drilling, done after the outside had been roughly finished. The bow-rotated drill was fitted with a small cylindrical bit of metal, probably copper, and worked with the aid of abrasive powder of finely ground quartz or similar. The far-reaching effect of the discovery of the bow-drill is borne out by the fact that this implement became the hieroglyphic sign for arts and crafts generally.

Stone vases of ancient Egypt are divided into five main groups according to material and shape. The most favoured material for the manufacture of vessels and luxury articles generally was, consistently, alabaster. It was used from pre-dynastic times, and remained in extensive use for small objects even after the introduction of softer stones. Egyptian alabaster was of the compact calcite variety, somewhat transluscient. It could not be scratched. The banded type is sometimes referred to as "onyx marble" (XVI).

In fact, from the Old Kingdom onwards, all other hard stones were considerably less utilised than in previous periods.

Pale blue anhydrite, worked into small vases, was used during Dynasty XII.

Other than cosmetic jars, most stone vases found were intended for funerary purposes, as they provided a more durable type of receptacle in the tomb equipment than pottery. For measuring liquids, a wide variety of special vessels, each with its own name, was made. There were containers for beer, wine, milk, oil, honey. Certain types of vessels served to measure grain and incense. Water-clocks (clepsydrae) from New Kingdom times were large stone bowls with high sides, in which the water drained away through small holes in the base.

SCULPTURE

Stone and ivory carvings exist from early predynastic times in Egypt. Objects have been found dating from the beginning of the dynastic age which show characteristics of later Egyptian art. Statuary was probably first made as part of the cult of kings who, upon death, became gods. Like many other royal prerogatives, this custom was gradually extended to the royal family, the court and finally the ruling class and its officials. Up to Dynasty VI, with few exceptions, the statue was insulated from danger in its serdab (Arabic: cellar), a special tomb. A magic ritual which the statue underwent ensured it being imbued with the spirit of the dead person.

Few statues, mostly on a small scale, remain from the Archaic or Thinite Period. Tombs for royalty and private persons during the Old Kingdom were increasingly built of stone, and numerous statues of kings and gods were made for their embellishment. The king was shown frontally posed, standing, invariably with the left leg advanced, or seated on a cubic block-like throne or chair. There is no suggestion of action or movement in these figures. Back pillars, reaching from base to shoulder, neck or head, were a more or less constant feature in Egyptian statuary. Whether this was done as a safeguard against splintering of the stone or had a symbolic purpose, is not clear.

A fixed canon of proportion and rigid iconography resulted in the summary execution of the body, emphasis of the musculature of the upper parts, with legs and ankles usually rendered in near-cubic shape, untapered, and with splayed toes of equal lengths. The greatest skill and art were devoted to the carving of the head, with features idealised to convey the essential god-head of the king (IV).

A feature of Old Kingdom tombs were figures of servants shown in a great variety of menial tasks of the kind they carried out during the life of the deceased (V). These figures were animated by magic so as to continue work for their master in the after-life. Since the idealistic conventions adhered to in carving statues of the mighty did not apply to these servant figures, a great deal of realism and movement was possible and often evident. So-called reserve heads (5) carved with a summary treatment of the planes of the face, always without a wig, were a short-lived Old Kingdom custom. Put in the actual burial chamber, they were presumably meant as substitute heads in the event of the destruction of the actual body.

Private statuary from the Old Kingdom followed conventions of royal sculpture (without, however, the idealised features bearing authority of divine kingship.) Many such figures, generally of painted limestone, were found in the mastabas or private tombs (mastaba: bench in Arabic) usually showing a man and wife either seated or standing, (VI) frontally

5) RESERVE HEAD OF A MEMBER OF THE COURT OF KING KHUFU (CHEOPS), DYNASTY IV

The Old Kingdom custom of using so-called reserve heads lasted only during the "Pyramid Dynasty." In their summary treatment of the planes of the face, they suggest an attempt to reproduce in a more permanent form the plaster masks modelled over the linen mummy-wrappings. They were almost certainly products of the royal workshops.

Married to a royal princess, the owner of this head was Treasurer to the king. A prominent nose and high, pointed cheekbones plus unusually shaped lips certainly create a feeling of a deliberate attempt at portraiture by an artist of outstanding talent.

posed and static. The third standard pose for statuary was that of the cross-legged squatting scribe, with a papyrus roll in his lap (6). Several statues of the deceased were commonly made for his tomb; in an extreme case, the number was over one hundred.

Relief carving in stone was an important part of the decoration and narration on walls of tombs. It is in this delicate shallow raised relief work (VII) that Egyptian art at its best can be seen. In time, because it could be easily damaged or usurped, this type of work was replaced by the more economic but less decorative sunk relief (VIII). In this uniquely Egyptian mode of carving design and modelling were cut below the surface-level. Strict artistic conventions in rendering the human figure were followed. The head was shown in profile, with the eye seen as if frontally, as well as the shoulders. The chest was arranged in three-quarter view, while the legs were shown in profile. Often, no distinction was made between left and right feet or hands. Proportions of the human body, however, adhered to a strict canon. Throughout Egyptian art, sculpture was its most forceful and characteristic aspect. During the later phase of the Old Kingdom, the court style of sculpture experienced a democratisation to the point of turning it into a "genre" style of more liveliness than that of preceding periods. With the political collapse at the end of Dynasty VI, artistic developments seem to have also come to a standstill.

Middle Kingdom sculpture, from Dynasty XI onwards, shows an uncompromising formalism. As in sculpture from the Old Kingdom, the figure was never quite freed from its matrix. The deceased was not any longer shown alert, eagerly striding forward, but often seemingly retired within a cloak, in a squatting position, or seated tailor-fashion, reducing the form of the body to a cuboid mass (IX). This newly introduced "block" type statue made its appearance as an ex voto. It had no funerary significance nor did it owe its inspiration to a royal prototype. Starting with Dynasty XII statues of private persons could be placed in the temple.

The arts of the Old Kingdom had been strongly infused with life and meaning by the ritual of the sun-cult. This belief began to decay in the early days of the Middle Kingdom and to be supplanted by the Osirian worship. In keeping with the new religious ideas, the importance of statues of the dead decreased, as did the size of such sculptures. No longer, as in the Old Kingdom, were they placed in the serdab, carefully kept away from sight. Instead, the temple statue, as ex voto, was displayed, to be seen and read by priests and visitors, and meant to receive offerings and participate in religious ceremonies.

Royal monumental sculpture, in the shape of Osirid pillars forming architectural elements of temples, were another aspect of a more restrained approach to the depiction of the king. In portraiture of the king from later Middle Kingdom times, the severity of the earlier phase became softened into melancholy introspection. A rare harmony of form and content in this period of Egyptian art was exemplified in the sphinxes and other sculptures of the last great king of Dynasty XII (10).

6) GREY GRANITE STATUE OF THE SCRIBE NAKHT, FIRST PROPHET OF AMUN — DYN. XVII

The last of the three standard poses for sculpture of human figures developed during the Old Kingdom, the seated scribe was usually shown with his writing implements. This theme became again particularly favoured in New Kingdom times.

Although basically in the tradition of ancient prototypes, papyrus scroll opened in the lap of the man sitting on his haunches, the style is quite different from that showing the alertly self-confident features of Old Kingdom sculpture. However, the loss of certain aspects of Old Kingdom sculpture is balanced by a gain in grace, technique and beauty in this style.

The elaborate wig, and pleated sleeves of the garment unable to conceal the fat rolls on the upper torso of this high official are, clearly, of a new age in art. His head is bent down under the weight of the god of writing, Thoth, in his shape as a baboon, dictating his maxims to the prophet.

The paintings from the tomb of this Scribe of the Temple of Amun, which are reproduced in most publications on Egyptian art, are important because their subject matter is taken from daily life; i.e. harvesting, vintage, hunting and fishing, as well as banqueting scenes with female orchestras, dancing girls as entertainers, and otherwise in attendance to the guests (XXX).

With few exceptions, the majority of figures were no longer shown with their hands fisted rigidly alongside the body but holding them flat. An impassive attitude seems conveyed in these figures, with their sad faces and heavy-lidded eyes (7 and 8).

While limestone was the material most widely used for Old Kingdom statuary, hard stones, without additional colouring but often very high polish, were now frequently employed.

For obvious reasons, little has remained of wooden sculptures in the round; the earliest surviving examples being three statues of a priest of Dynasty V and his wife.

Middle Kingdom art seems to have been produced of circumstances shaped by the disastrous political events preceding it. In royal portraiture, it was less the divine god-king that was depicted than the forceful ruler, concerned with impressing the beholder with the awe due the terrestrial majesty. A massive, brooding quality is a characteristic of these sculptures, with faces displaying a heavy frowning expression (9).

Often crudely done wooden figures and groups were in use until the end of Dynasty XII replacing the lively servant figures of stone or wood of the Old Kingdom, and also taking over the function of painted reliefs.

While at the beginning of dynastic Egypt artists were, generally, totally anonymous members of a team in company with jewellers, joiners and smiths, several names of artists from the end of the Middle Kingdom have survived.

The next clearly defined and materially best represented period of Egyptian sculpture is that of the New Kingdom. Generally, it is distinguished from that of earlier periods by a wide variety within the conventional styles. In parts this was based on the radically changing trends of civilisation brought on by the Hyksos occupation during the Second Intermediate Period. With Egyptian expansion under Tuthmosis III began a phase of development affecting all parts of life. Taste was influenced by foreign tributes and resources. Military service abroad widened the horizons of people. The taste of art patrons turned towards the elegant and luxurious, a fact evidenced in all art during the period. Official art tended towards the grandiose and complacent, while that made for private owners often was of a personal and intimate quality.

7) PINK QUARTZITE STATUE OF SI-KAHIKA
A striking portrayal of old age, this statue displays the impassivity that is one of the hallmarks of sculpture of the Middle Kingdom. Showing an exceptional degree of individuality, this is, most likely, an actual portrait. Columns of carved texts along the front of the long kilt, as shown here, representing offering formulae, were possible during the Middle Kingdom. In preceding times, strictures had limited the location for inscriptions to the base, seat or back pillar of statues.

Long kilts had been worn by officials from Dynasty III onwards. This example is, nevertheless, a fashion of the later XIIth Dynasty, with its upper edge reaching above the navel of Si-Kahika. Hands held flat upon his lap is a detail shown in royal statuary for the first time in a portrait of Amen-em-het III.

8) DANCING DWARFS OF IVORY

Mounted on small circular pedestals whose holes correspond to those in the figures, these could be actuated by strings, to revolve and pirouette. Possibly these figurines were toys. The intensity and liveliness of their different poses and facial expressions places them into the Middle Kingdom expressionistic style often called brutal realism. The one on the right has a combined vertical and horizontal furrowing of the brow, which is also slightly indicated in the sculpture from the same period, of Si-Kahika (7), the only other Middle Kingdom statue generally known to display this aspect of old age. Wearing a bandolier or necklaces of huge globular beads, they clap their hands in tune to the music of the sacred dance such persons were usually engaged in, greeting the sun-god with their acrobatics. Pygmies first appeared in Old Kingdom relief scenes of goldsmithing, where they handle the finished ornaments, assembling and storing them. Ptah, the patron of craftsmen, sometimes appears in the form of the dwarf Patek. They were employed as personal valets of the royal family and high court officials. A traveller in the service of King Pepy II, last king of Dynasty VI, is instructed to "bring the pygmy alive, prosperous and healthy to perform the dances of the god and to amuse your master . . ." The legend, of a much later date, of pygmies fighting cranes grew so vividly in Mediterranean lands that it served as a theme for numerous paintings and mosaics in Greek and Roman art.

9) GRANITE HEAD OF KING SESOSTRIS III

Prominent cheekbones, heavy-lidded eyes and a strong jaw all combine to reflect a man of rugged determination; a vigorous, stern and somewhat disillusioned monarch. The only far-reaching military expedition in the north as far as Samaria recorded from the Middle Kingdom was led in person by this king. From the southern end of the Second Cataract at Semna, which formed the frontier of Egypt during the Middle Kingdom, Sesostris III founded six fortresses northwards to unite Upper and Lower Egypt and Nubia into a powerful and easily defensible province. The king wears the Nemes, the royal striped headdress. The extremely high polish of the hard stone was given to many statues of the time, differing from **Old Kingdom sculptures, mostly carved of softer stones and, usually, painted.**

10) BLACK GRANITE SPHINX OF KING AMEN-EM-HET III

The son of Sesostris III, Amen-em-het III was hailed as a superhuman who illuminated the earth more than the sun. This attitude is expressed in much of the realistic portrait sculpture of him, such as this and two other sphinxes. Colossal statuary of this kind acted as emphasis of the central power and towering stature of the ruler. The unity of style and expression in statues from the late part of the Middle Kingdom ends with the reign of this king, fading into a cultural decline which affected intimately the arts in general. The usual type of Egyptian sphinx has the body of a lion and the head of the reigning monarch wearing the Nemes with its lappets, while this sculpture and two companion pieces bear the mane of a lion. The monumental leonine, regal character places this type apart from other similar sculptures, while the bold modelling of the animal and the human musculature, fully integrated into each other, create a rarely surpassed force and impressiveness. The artist has seized upon the salient features of the king and brought them out in an autocratic display of accentuated cheekbones, pouches under the eyes and near the corners of the mouth, and the slight upward tilt of the king's chin. The sculpture was usurped by Ramesses II and others who cut their own ugly cartouche inscriptions in it. On Amen-em-het III's own name-cartouche appears a similar sphinx with a lion's mane. The Egyptian word for sphinx, shesp-ankh when referred to androcephalic (male-headed) lions, meant "living stone." It represented royal power and indomitability in battle, and was placed flanking the temple of the king for protection of the sanctuary. Sometimes gods themselves, incarnate in fantastic animals, were represented as sphinxes defending their own house of worship, such as the ram-headed sphinxes associated with Amun at Karnak. Responsible for far-reaching developments carried out in the Fayum, Amen-em-het III was deified and worshipped in the area until two thousand years after his death.

11) EBONY STATUE OF MERI-PTAH, MASTER OF THE STABLES TO AMENOPHIS III

From the earlier part of the New Kingdom, when great attention was paid to depicting details of clothing and hairstyles, the sculpture is made of Sudanese ebony. A number of objects in this type of wood, particularly small-scale human figures (18), come from the time of Amenophis's III reign.

The over-idealising of early New Kingdom sculpture is very much evident in the carving of the features, but the manneristic tendencies, to come to a full development in the arts during the reign of Amenophis' son Akhenaten, are also apparent.

The man wears a four-row necklace of truncated cones of beaten gold with large holes and perforated bases. Each pair of cones is soldered along the medial seams.

This is the shebyu or "Collar of Honour," given in special ceremonies by the king for a particular service, as seen in many reliefs. The awarding of the "Collar of Honour" dates to Old Kingdom times. In the later part of that era when the power of the ruling class attained almost that of the king, heralding the soon-to-come collapse of the Old Kingdom, feudal lords emulated the king by awarding followers with gold ornaments. In a relief from the tomb of a son of King Men-kau-Re; builder of the third pyramid at Giza, the owner presents gold necklaces to dancers who entertain him.

In somewhat later usage of the New Kingdom, strings of gold rings (vs. this where rows of gold cones are fashioned into one unit) are represented as being hung around the necks of persons honoured at festivals or state occasions.

These tangible tokens of recognition by the king were also of great intrinsic value, in a time before the invention of coinage.

New Kingdom sculpture encompasses work of impassive expression (Xa, 11), of realistic nature (12) or a formal style (13). It was produced on a huge scale (14) as well as in minute size (15). Tender emotion was expressed (16, XI) and idealised features (XII) juxtaposed against stark realism verging on abstraction of external human characteristics (17). The traditional rendering of sculptured features was practised (XII), albeit sometimes within the artistic canons of Amarna art (18). Expressionistic art also had its place in sculpture of the period (19) as did the intimate (20, 21, 22).

The sculpture of the later New Kingdom follows the style set by Ramesses II in the numerous statues he had made of himself (23), typically on a monumental scale. Some works from the period, however, show the retention of features current during the Amarna Period (24).

13) GREYWACKE STATUE OF TUTHMOSIS III, "HERO OF THE NEW KINGDOM"

After the long denial of his right to the throne by Queen Hatshepsut and much belated ascension, this king was to become one of the greatest, if not the most outstanding, ruler of ancient Egypt's history. Her fortunes soared under his reign and she reached her greatest political expansion ever.

New Kingdom statuary of the early part often emulated Old Kingdom prototypes, surpassing it in technical perfection but, perhaps because of this latter fact, lacks the vitality of the older masterpieces. Details of regalia and clothing, rigidity of pose and highly idealised features adhere to ancient tradition.

The king's throne-name (prenomen) is carved within the cartouche on the belt buckle of his kilt: Men-kheper-Re, i. e. "The form-of-Re-abides." The statue has a plinth on its back inscribed with the full (five in all) royal names and titles.

14) BLACK GRANITE STATUE OF THE GOD PTAH OF MEMPHIS

This over-life sized sculpture was dedicated by Amenophis III to the god "beautiful of face," patron of royalty and member of the Memphite triad. Considered locally the creator of the world, Ptah, thought to be the inventor of craftsmen, became also the patron of craftsmen; his High Priest was called "Lord of the Master-Craftsmen."

Mummiform, he holds two ankh signs, as well as the sceptres of stability and duration (DJED pillar) and of power (WAS). Ousekh collar, ceremonial beard and wide bracelets complete the accoutrements. The head is covered by the close-fitting skull cap traditionally worn by Ptah.

12) LIMESTONE STATUE OF NEFER-TITI

The queen whose name translates into "The-beautiful-woman-has-come" is shown within the still exaggerated terms of the later Amarna Period. The artistic canon of the period of elongating the head was extended beyond the members of the court. The hint of tired illusion in the lines from the corners of the mouth (another tradition of Amarna art) creates an all too realistic impact on the beholder of a woman who was the mother of six living and a number of still-born children. It was said that witch doctors aided Nefer-titi in child-birth by narrowing the skulls of the newborn.

The theory to explain the distorted elongation of heads from the Amarna Period by deliberate cranial deformation is not borne out by material evidence. In the case of one of Akhenaten's and Nefer-titi's daughters, her head is shown with the fashionably distorted cranium, while the same princess later as the wife of Tut-ankh-amun is shown with a perfectly normal head and neck.

As in the celebrated polychromed bust of the queen (in Berlin), here, too, the artist has achieved a superb counterbalance between the long forward curving neck and the back sloping of the head. In contrast to the many idealised versions of her, the queen's face and figure are rendered as realistically as the style permitted.

15) STATUE OF A SERVANT GIRL CARRYING A JAR —BOXWOOD—NEW KINGDOM

An oversized unguent jar, pivoted by a peg, is carried by a lovely slim girl with Nubian features, the sidelock of youth on the left of her head and a modest gilded belt around her loins. She wears a Bes-amulet on a necklace.

An unsymmetrical balance, by giving the upper part a contraposto which is repeated in the pose of the legs, is the result of attempting to show the anatomical tensions of a person carrying a disproportionally heavy load. In this, the figure, along with two others known (and presumably by the same carver) is unique. It is only 5 1/2" high.

16) CLASPED HANDS OF FINE-GRAINED LIGHT BROWN QUARTZITE

The carving from an Amarna group-statue is a superb echo of the intimacy which distinguishes many representations of Akhenaten and his family. No other period of Egyptian antiquity has as vivid examples of that tendency as that of the king later referred to as "the criminal of Amarna."

The piece is carved entirely in the round. The D-shaped impressions for the nails possibly indicate inlay with coloured glass or stone (a foot of the same provenance shows this to have been practised). The left hand, more slender than the other, may have been a woman's of younger age. In group sculpture of Akhenaten and his wife or one of his elder daughters, it is usually the latter who grasps the king's hand rather than vc. vs. The sculptor responsible for this piece was unquestionably a master of his art.

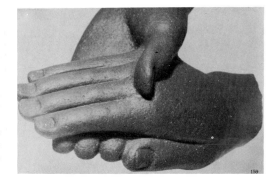

17) LIMESTONE SUNK RELIEF FRAGMENT OF AKHENATEN

The deliberate distortions of the early Amarna style, based partly on the king's own physical appearance, are evident in this carving: cadaverous cheeks, protruding lips, pendulous jaw, long and narrow forehead, scrawny neck seemingly barely able to support the head, slanted eyes, and earlobes extended to the point of reducing them to rings of flesh. It was presumably part of a relief showing the king in a gesture of adoration of the Aten. The varying depths of the carving create a strong effect of light and shadow. The piece is obviously the work of a master-sculptor of the court.

18) WOODEN STATUE OF THE LADY TUTY

It comes from a group of six small statues of women in the same late Dynasty XVII tomb that was the common burial place of all of them. The little ebony figure, clad in a transparent gown exposing the left breast, originally wore gilt sandals (outline visible on base). The huge faience studs in the ears are gilt, as is the perfume cone atop the relatively oversized wig, carved in two pieces and attached by wooden plugs. The cone with a movable ring is one of only two actual plastic examples known. Some black and white paint for the eyes is still extant.

Untitled, Tuty was presumably one of the royal concubines. This information is based on other objects from the tomb bearing royal names (Amenophis III was known to have had a palace in the area). Given Amarna provenance by one scholar, the base inscription referring to gods outside the monotheistic era would indicate either an earlier or later production for this piece. The realism of the Nubian features of this lovely female, albeit within a traditional format, is remarkable.

19) SUNK RELIEF OF HERDSMAN AND GOAT

The discoloured limestone shows no trace of the original paint. A genre scene of greatly expressive impact, it is carved with unusual boldness and competence. A goat with its wrinkled muzzle nibbles on a tuft of grass. The unkempt herdsman with a short beard reaching to the ears, sunken cheeks, protruding belly with outward pointing navel and a crook with bag over his shoulders conforms to the Amarna tradition of figure rendering. The arrangement of the human body is much more naturalistic than the usually strictly adhered-to canons of Egyptian art in relief and painting. The type of man shown here is known from Middle Kingdom art representations of desert-tribes herdsmen.

20) AKHENATEN AND DAUGHTER — PORTION OF SUNK RELIEF SHOWING THE ROYAL FAMILY

From a private chapel, the whole stela shows the Aten in the top centre, its beneficient rays ending traditionally in hands, the ones in front of the royal faces holding an ankh sign. It is done in the style of the Amarna conversation piece from the early part of the reign.

Even in this portion of the relief can be seen the psychological relationship, which creates the overall-unity of the picture. Akhenaten's daughter points towards where her mother sits with one girl on her lap and one standing within her left arm.

The graduated depth of the carving gives a strongly plastic effect to the face and figure of the king and child, as well as, particularly (not seen here) the seat cushion.

A telling example of depicting intimate scenes from Akhenaten's family life, unprecedented and not repeated in Egyptian art, this is perhaps the technically most successful of that type.

21) AKHENATEN AS SPHINX — AMARNA PERIOD

From the early period of the reign of "the heretic king," the sunk relief depicts him in the shape of a sphinx, its body elongated in accordance with artistic traditions from the Amarna Period. The human head wears the Afnet headdress rather than the more common Nemes (royal headdress of striped design) as seen on sphinxes of Egyptian kings generally. From the Aten sun-disk emanate its life-giving rays, terminating in hands as usual, the one in front of the royal face holding out the ankh-sign of life. The rays reaching over the back part of the sphinx's body are not actually carved but rather painted only. Offerings on stands are placed in front of the figure, while the king's hands hold up libation vessels to the Aten. The inscriptions above refer to the Aten, Akhenaten, and his wife, Nefer-titi.

23) UPPER PART OF BLACK GRANITE STATUE OF RAMESSES II

Seated on a cubic throne with high back, Ramesses is shown with his distinctly shaped nose. In the mummy of the king this characteristic is clearly borne out. That it should also be indicated in official portraiture of the living ruler implies a deliberate attempt at truthful rendering of the sitter.

The earlobes are only partly pierced. The Buto cobra on his brow, Ramesses wears the Blue Crown or "Battle Helmet" (Khepresh) frequently shown from the New Kingdom on, and first worn by rulers of the preceding Hyksos dynasty.

The name-cartouches are surmounted by the Ibes crown of two ostrich feathers flanking a solar disk. The ousekh necklace covers the top part of the apparently gossamer-thin pleated garment, leaving only the right arm free. The right hand holds the ceremonial crock, the left a stave of office.

The lower part of the long aproned kilt has a centrally placed hieroglyphic inscription as does the plinth at the back. To either side of the king's leg is a small-scale carving of his favourite wife Nefer-ta-ri and son Amun-her-khopechef.

24) LIMESTONE RELIEF OF SETHOS I, 2nd KING OF DYNASTY XIX

The father of Ramesses II, Sethos I was very active in restoring Egyptian authority in Nubia and Western Asia, and rebuilding temples. The most outstanding of his latter achievements was the Temple of Osiris at Abydos which contains a list of kings of Egypt arranged in chronological order. Of the (four) major original sources for tracing lengths and sequence of the reigns of rulers of Egypt, the one initiated by Sethos I remains the most famous and well-preserved.

The relief is most outstanding of its type, with infinite attention paid to details of the tightly curled wig and beard, (attachment straps not carved). An uraeus with a head on either end of its body is elegantly coiled around the diadem, tied at the back of the head. Sethos's nose is of similar shape to that of his famous son.

The naos, or small shrine of the period was fashioned of wood, or sometimes harder materials.

The Libyan Period produced, by a school of palace artists, skilfully worked objects of bronze, silver, gold, as well as of electrum on a small scale. Some of these have never been surpassed in their elegant proportions of bodies and accoutrements (XIV). Monumental sculpture was not a feature of this period. Profoundly pious offering figures were carved during Dynasty XXIII, whose kings seem to have been related to the Bubastite rulers, bearing names such as the latter did.

The celebrated realism, particularly in the depiction of old age, commonly associated with the Saite Period, was strongly evident in sculpture of the preceding, Kushite, Period (XV).

Renewed splendour, political and spiritual renaissance during the Saite Period, were coupled with artistic revival based on inspirations from Old and Middle Kingdom art, and a direct adoption of the artistic achievements of Dynasty XXV, unequalled since Ramesside times. Native Egyptian sculptors, having worked under the ruling southern conquerors of Kushite times, acted under new and very vigorous influences, carrying this artistic quality over into the next dynasty. The idealistic, academic art, with its particularly high quality surface work in objects of hard stones, is occasionally termed as lacking inner conviction. Nevertheless, the profound observation of prototypes which produced Saite sculpture, created works of great aesthetic appeal. It was in its culmination an artistic revival based on antiquarianism.

The noticeable increase in the use of harder stones for sculpture, particularly schist and basalt, that had characterised works from the Saite Period, continued until the end of Ptolemaic times. The traditional skill of the Egyptian artist of former periods is evident in these carvings.

In carvings of the human figure, from Dynasty XXVI onwards, a tripartite construction of the torso is common. It was divided into the separate elements of abdomen, rib cage and breast, with a deeply depressed navel area. Faultlessly executed, the high polish on the majority of these figures gives them, nevertheless, a feeling of lifelessness. Except for the traditional pose and simplicity of dress, little in these works is reminiscent of previous periods.

The last phase of purely Pharaonic art is that of the Ptolemaic Period. Some brilliant portraiture dates from the time. Greek naturalism in modelling of the figure was greatly evident from Dynasty XXX onwards. In the earlier part of the fourth century B. C., a superficial mingling of Greek and Egyptian forms in sculpture produced a slightly erotic effect (25). It was either a somewhat pedantic repetition of the old Egyptian types, or else in its other main branch, of pure Greek form. Foreshortening was occasionally mastered in relief carving. A peculiarity of Ptolemaic sculpture are the pointed breasts and prominent abdominal muscles. Another feature of fourth century B. C. art was a type of unusual relief carvings surmounted by a torus moulding.

During the early rule of the Roman Empire, Egypt's artists were commissioned to create works of art in the native style. The traditional Egyptian styles, however, gradually became so permeated with Western conceptions as to completely disappear in the third century A. D. With it also died out the use of hard stones for sculpture (26).

In the Coptic era, sandstone and limestone were used for the bulk of carved work. Excepting the ankh-sign and a few other pre-Christian symbols of religious context, style and subject matter show no trace of Pharaonic Egypt. Early Coptic architectural relief decoration is drawn from Hellenistic subject matter, with figures in high relief, friezes, in niches, etc. as well as plant ornamentation and geometric designs (27). Tombstones were another specific feature of Coptic sculpture, but neither in their relief work nor inscription have they seemingly evolved from the Egyptian funerary stelae.

From the beginning of the introduction of Christian themes, they are often mingled with pagan ones in Coptic art. The frequently used group of Mary and the infant Jesus thus is closely reminiscent of Isis suckling Horus-the-child.

For obvious reasons, little of wooden figure carving, from door panels and friezes, has survived. The same degree of quality of workmanship seen in other aspects of Coptic sculpture, is evident in the few extant pieces of wooden carving.

Colour was an essential part of Coptic sculpture. As it has generally disappeared, the impact of an art style which, as a rule, lacked modelling and finesse of detail, is greatly reduced.

25) BLACK GRANITE BUST FRAGMENT OF PTOLEMAIC QUEEN
The lappets of the wig rest on the breasts, which are covered by a very thin tunic. The unusual arrangement of three uraei on the queen's forehead has its first precedent in statues of Amenhotep III and his queen, Dynasty XVIII. As the sacred vulture is carved atop the hair with wings spreading down behind the queen's ears, the talons at the back of the head holding the SHEN sign for eternity, the central uraeus represents an adaptation of the vulture's head. The headdress is that of reigning queens. No actual example of this is extant but a number of representations in tomb paintings, one of Cleopatra VII among them, have survived. They seem to have been made of gold elements combined together into a flexible head covering.

The squat modius on top of the headdress here is missing. It would have carried the solar disk flanked by two tall feathers.

Formal elements of Egyptian sculpture such as the plinth at the back and the tripartition of the hair contrast with Greek influence, manifested in the natural, unstylised lines of the lips and sunken cheekbones.

27) HORUS MOUNTED — SANDSTONE — FIFTH C. A.D.

Having undergone a transformation in symbol, spirit and treatment from the great falcon-headed god of the Pharaonic pantheon, Horus is here depicted as a Roman cavalryman. The god trampling the crocodile underfoot is common in Egyptian mythology and essentially symbolizes the triumph of good over evil. The arrangement of Horus clad in armour began in the second C. A. D.

The horse's head turning towards the rider creates a movement in depth. In stone-working generally, Coptic art tended to lag behind developments in other parts of the Byzantine Empire, as a rule rather crudely done, somewhat akin to folk art. Bulging eyes are one of the hallmarks of Coptic art.

FRESCO PAINTING OF THE VIRGO LACTANS — THIRD C. A. D.

In this period a few Christian themes of Alexandrian origin, began to appear in art, Alexandria (and Antioch) being the centres with the largest number of early Christians. Pagan themes were the transparent subject matter, overlaid with Christianised details.

Isis here thus becomes the nursing Mother Mary. But it is still clearly the infant Horus or Harpokrat s with his hieroglyphic symbol of childhood (sidelock, forefinger on mouth), as Jesus, on her lap. He wears an amulet (of Bes?) around his neck, shoes and socks, while the virgin is bedecked with rings, bracelet and bead necklace. Details like these might be termed typical of the preoccupations of folk art.

The folds of the drapery, reaching over the high back of the chair (throne?) and extending along the sides to the seat, are reduced to mere lines indicating the fabric by a few vertical brushstrokes.

The virgin's tunic-like garment of Roman type is held in place by means of a fibula below the right shoulder.

Sharp contours, and figure proportions of clumsiness are associated with Coptic art, particularly in tiny breasts, set too high, angular forms and conventional treatment of the hair.

26) BUST OF A CAESAR— IMPERIAL PORPHYRY— C. A.D. 310

From Late Roman Empire days, this bust is executed in abstracted realistic forms, with its head twisting on its axis. The style of the face is sometimes called the "cult of imperial ugliness."

In A.D. 296 Alexandria had revolted against Roman rule and, along with other rebellious centres of the Empire, was put in charge of a determined military leader. The man portrayed is either Maximinus Daia, or Licinius. Several porphyry portraits (quarries were at Aswan, Sinai and the Eastern Desert) which have survived of these eastern rulers bear out character of iron will and strength. The very last examples of Egyptian sculpture, albeit already almost completely westernised in concept, they also signalled the end of the use of hard stones for the purpose.

Minor details still point to the ultimate artistic origin of the men who produced such works. The cloak folds are caught on the shoulder by means of a fibula, in itself in use (not by native Egyptians) only from Roman times.

METALS, METAL TOOLS AND WEAPONS

The ancient Near East and Egypt can be mapped by a study of the geological strata. Copper for Egyptian consumption was obtained from the Eastern Desert. A particular region in Syria was known to the authors of the Amarna Letters as the "Land of copper." More important for the import of copper were the mines of Cyprus, a name derived from the Late Latin term cuprum, hence for the metal. Whether or not copper was mined, and possibly also smelted, in Sinai is still a matter of dispute. During the Badarian Period copper was used for small implements like needles and borers. From late predynastic times until the Middle Kingdom copper remained the most commonly used metal for weapons, tools, figurines, jewellery and objects for domestic use. From dynastic times on, it was plentiful, and its use obviously contributed largely to the dynamic development of the material culture of Egypt. From Dynasty I on, it was made into ceremonial objects; royal statues representing gods were then made of this material. Copper overlay was used in temple decoration. The earliest surviving example of copper sculpture is from Dynasty VI. From this time until the New Kingdom no copper statues survive. Due to the scarcity of the metal, objects were melted down and the material re-used. As early as mid-second millenium B. C., the hollow pipes used as bellows in metal working were replaced by foot-operated ones. Moulds used in the production of flat metal tools and weapons have been found, dating from the Middle Bronze Age on. Many tomb paintings show scenes from metal working; from them the various methods can be clearly observed. Scenes of crude metal and tools being weighed before and after use by the workmen are the subject of many tomb paintings. Significantly, the balance used is of a type otherwise depicted only in vignettes showing the "Weighing of the Heart" from the "Book of the Dead." In trial records, theft of metal figures prominently. Models of metal tools have occasionally been found as part of funerary equipment. A rarity, and of great interest for the purpose of dating are tools marked with royal cartouche-names.

Bronze was produced in abundance in the Near East but the common use in Egypt of this alloy of tin and copper took place much later than elsewhere. It seems not to have been known before the Middle Kingdom. From then on it was regularly used for the manufacture of tools and weapons, which continued to be made of it long after the introduction of, and, for a while alongside with, iron. As yet it is not clear whether the manufactured alloy was imported or the alloying done in Egyptian workshops. An insignificant amount of tin was found in

Egypt. The richest sources for it were in Europe and not, presumably, open to the Near East until Phoenician seafarer times. Syria and India also produced tin so that these areas could have provided the material. In the extensive hieroglyphic texts for minerals, tin is nowhere identifiable with certainty. Bronze was shaped in three different main ways: by mould-casting, extensively from New Kingdom times onwards by the cire-perdue method, and for objects made of sheet metal, repousse work. The cire-perdue or lost wax method had been practised in the Near East since the end of the fourth millenium B. C. Objects from Nakada II or Gerzean Period were found to be cast by this method and it would seem to have been the invention of the Egyptian metal worker of that period.

Except for meteoric iron which, because of its "heavenly" origin was early invested with magical properties, iron is not found in a pure state. The Egyptians knew and used meteoric iron as early as approx. 3000 B. C., i.e. during the Thinite or Archaic Period. The credit for the discovery of separating iron from its oxides goes to the Hittites. The spread of this knowledge occurred on the collapse of their empire and the resultant wandering of the Sea Peoples. Of these, Philistine warriors were buried with weapons, tools and jewellery made of iron.

Iron had such great advantages over bronze that its use spread rapidly. In Egypt, the forging of iron lagged behind that of other Near Eastern countries. Two basic methods for working iron were forging and casting. Very few objects have been found from dynastic times; most were analyzed as meteoric. An indicator of the scarcity of this metal even at the time of the New Kingdom are the extremely small, few pieces that were found in Tutankh-amun's tomb as compared to the great number and weight of gold objects. The use of iron increased from Dynasty XVIII onwards, but only from Ptolemaic times was it manufactured into tools. Household implements such as knives, flesh hooks etc. of iron were common from Roman times.

The weapons of Egypt, from the beginning of the Dynastic Period to the Middle Kingdom, were identical with those of their African and Palestinian neighbours. As a result of Asiatic contacts, military equipment experienced some changes. The change-over from flint to metal tools was considerably slower in Egypt than in other countries. Daggers were made of flint, copper, bronze, iron, and, for ceremonial purposes, occasionally of bone, ivory, or a combination of precious metals, some beautifully decorated. Daggers were used from predynastic times on, although examples from even as early as the Old Kingdom are extremely rare. In the funerary equipment of some royal persons, daggers with solid gold sheaths were included, some with cloisonne or granule work, or several methods of decoration combined. The dagger was so similar to an ordinary double-bladed knife that very often the distinction between the two cannot be made. Some dagger forms in use in Egypt were triangular or ogival. Cheek pieces of daggers were round, made of bone or ivory, or stone (2). During the second half of the Middle Bronze Age the very narrow dagger was replaced by a broader blade, resembling a leaf in shape. The blade thus had to be strengthened and was often given one or more prominent spines. Characteristic of daggers of the Late Bronze Age are blade and hilt made in one piece. Hilts were often studded with wood, bone or precious metals.

The defense armour of the Egyptian soldier until the New Kingdom was a rectangular shield of toughened leather, stretched over a wooden brace, with a curve at the top. During the later New Kingdom mail coats of small bronze plates rivetted to leather jerkins appeared. From Roman times came a suit of armour consisting of three pieces of crocodile skin, one for each shoulder, one for the neck and the head. Personal weapons of the Egyptian soldier were daggers, swords, spears, halberds and lances. The bow was used in all periods. It remained a symbol of a warring nation. The phrase "The nine bows" was used to designate enemy peoples in remembrance of the nine nations whom the first kings of Egypt overcame with their warlike strength.

Axes with wooden handles were in use from prehistoric times, and were made of a variety of materials, such as stone and, later, metal. The variety of shapes depended largely on the material used, and the method of hafting.

The main function of the axe was for food working. The standard procedure for sharpening axes and adzes from Neolithic times on was with the aid of sand and water. Pressure flaking was the commonly used technique for the manufacture of these tools.

Spears were replicas of the javelin in shape but heavier and used with a thrusting, rather than throwing, movement. Leaf-shape was the standard form for a long time. The spear was fitted to the shaft by means of a long tang with a rear hook to ensure secure attachment and a spike-like butt fitted to the shaft and head by means of an end curve and the metal spiral band. The latter encircled the handle, fastened to it by nails. When the spear was not in use, this butt on the spear rest was a means of sticking the weapon into the ground. Also, the butt made a useful weapon in itself in particular circumstances.

Bronze spear heads of leaf-shape, with midrib ending in a round, hollow socket for insertion of the haft formed a standard type and remained in use, with minor variations, throughout Egypt's ancient history.

2) ALABASTER BUTT FOR DAGGER
of ball-shape, the "Mycenean" type. It has two equidistant wall-perforations in mid-body: butts for dagger handles had such perforations on either two or three sides of the wall for insertion into, and attachment to, the handle. C. 1359.

3) COPPER ADZEHEAD
hammered, with a straight, thin neck and bevelled cutting edge; the plane of the blade is at right angles to the haft hole. Before the introduction of the saw, the main function of the adze was for trimming timber. C. 1251. Adzes were flat and heavy cutting tools, made of stone or metal, and distinguished from the axe by an asymmetrical cross-section.

Copper battle axeheads of the general Near Eastern scalloped or epsilon-shaped type, developed in the early Middle Bronze Age, first known as "eye axe." Later the form was elongated and the eyes made smaller, into the "duck-bill" type. As all battle axes, this type was of the shaft hole variety.

The sword was an object of warfare as well as prestige. Its blades were made for slashing or thrusting, or both. It differs from the dagger by its greater length. The blade often had incised decoration in the form of a lotus stem or birds, etc. During the Second Intermediate Period a curved scimitar-like sword with a handle in one piece, called Khepesh, was introduced patterned on Western Asiatic models.

As with knives made of flint, blades of metal were produced in a great variety of shapes and sizes. The greatest expansion of the manufacture of metal tools and implements occurred during the Roman Period.

METAL OBJECTS OTHER THAN TOOLS AND WEAPONS

The introduction of copper, and later bronze, meant aside from the large-scale production of weapons and tools fashioned from these metals, also the making of a variety of domestic utensils. Household vessels of metal were put to a twofold purpose in this precoinage age: they provided barter items for their owners along with the second important commodity for this, textiles. The only place in ancient Egypt where silver and bronze coins were known to have been struck was at the Greek commercial settlement of Naucratis. Toilet articles, such as mirrors (4), tweezers, pins and razors were commonly made of metal. During the New Kingdom, razors were made in the shape of a sharp-edged miniature axe fixed to a wooden handle and rotated by the fingers. Tweezers were employed for the removal of hair as well as the extraction of thorns. Ladies removed their body hair daily with the help of pumice stone.

Metalwork was mainly controlled by the government; the arsenal at Memphis having been the oldest collective workshop in the world. There were references to the "metalsmiths of Amun" and the "smelters of Ptah" in texts. For small-scale objects, suitable open moulds were used. A modern version of the ancient Egyptian foot-operated bellows employed in metalworking was found in the Sudan. Small bronze objects for cosmetic and other purposes were made in abundance during the Roman Period.

An untold number of bronze statues of deities and sacred animals date to the Saite Period. Made as temple offerings and, although mass-produced, superb technical expertise and knowledge of anatomy is invariably evident in these figures. Particularly popular were the bronze votive cats as well as falcons. For the extensive animal cemeteries built during the Late Period, hollow-cast bronzes were manufactured to serve as coffins for mummified cats, birds, apes, asps, etc.

Very important as one of the incarnation animals of the god Thoth, the ibis was frequently fashioned (II) with the legs, hind part, neck and beak of bronze, while the body was made of wood, sometimes gilded, or of alabaster. Thoth being the local god of Hermopolis in Middle Egypt, the town had large ibis cemeteries.

The ancestor of the fibula, the pin was most commonly used to fasten garments, more rarely for the hair. No Egyptian type of dress is known until Roman times which would have called for the use of a pin. However, a great number of toggle pins were found in Hyksos tombs.

Aside from metal, pins were also made of bone. As a highly important cultural indicator, the extremely variable decorative heads on such pins have afforded many clues to archaeology.

4) BRONZE MIRROR WITH HATHOR-HEAD HANDLE

Mirrors were in use in Egypt from early times onwards, made of circular flat metal disks with a polished surface for reflection. Aside from their use as an all-important article of toilet, they were thought to have some magical powers as well (as does the mirror in some African fetish figures).

The decoration of mirror surfaces began after Dynasty XXI; ritually significant scenes were sometimes incised upon them. Handles, fitted over the tang, were made of metal, wood, faience or ivory, shaped often as a Hathor-head or a figure of Bes, a papyrus column or a club, or a female figure supporting the mirror with outstretched arms. The cross-pieces were sometimes decorated with two protective falcon figures. A cult ritual for the goddesses Hathor and Mut was the offering of two mirrors. Kings are represented on the walls of temples of Hathor in such offering ceremonies.

Some mirrors such as this were made specifically as votive offerings. This piece confirms that Thoth was also offered mirrors. The incised scene shows the god of writing presenting offering-hieroglyphs ("All" with two WAS sceptres for power, and an ankh sign for life) to the goddess of truth, Ma'at, her emblematic feather on her head. The ibis-headed god wears the royal shendyt (all-over pleated kilt) with the bull's tail sown to it, another kingly regalia. Offered by a gatekeeper to Thoth-Djehuti at the sanctuary of Hermopolis, the mirror's inscription implores the "Twice-Great Lord of Hermopolis" to give "life, power, health, and a great and good old age" to him, New-Djehuti = "He-belongs-to-Thoth."

Traces of gold leaf on this Ptolemaic or Roman Period piece are visible. The wooden handle is surmounted by a double Hathor-head with characteristic upturned curls and cow ears.

PRECIOUS METALS

The immense gold deposits within Egypt herself were the richest in the ancient world. A contemporary Near Eastern proverb spoke of "gold as dust in the land of Egypt." The principal region for mining gold was the Eastern Desert, with traces of gold working in many other places. The ancient prospectors seem to have been thorough in their exploitation, since modern investigation did not turn up any workable deposits that had been overlooked. By Dynasty XIX, the more accessible sources were exhausted, and mines located further into the desert had to be worked (XXVIII).

Much of the gold, so lavishly used in arts and crafts, as well as a diplomatic weapon (in the New Kingdom), reached Egypt as tribute from the Lower Sudan and Nubia and, when the latter was incorporated into the Egyptian empire, was directly worked there. Many reliefs and paintings show gold being offered in the form of granules (in red leather bags), or melted into larger ingots or crude rings, strung up loop-in-loop fashion.

The earliest small gold objects extant, mostly beads, are from the Gerzean (Nakada II) Period of pre-dynastic Egypt. That the ancient goldsmith was perfectly capable of working precious metals into objects of any size, is borne out by the gold coffin of Tut-ankh-amun, which weighs over 300 lbs. The ancient tomb robbers concentrated their efforts mainly on gold objects, a

"Book of buried heads and precious treasures" greatly aiding them. Of the frequently depicted gold bowls, figure sculpture and gold masks, very little remains. The surviving examples of goldsmith's works are, for the most part, personal jewellery worn by both sexes.

Impurities in Egyptian gold were mainly of silver. If this content reaches 20% it becomes electrum, a pale amber-coloured alloy. Any higher content makes the whiteness of the metal indistinguishable from silver. The purity of gold seems to have been occasionally tested (Amarna Letters) by casting it into the furnace; the re-emerging pieces sometimes turned out to weigh less than before the process. This indicates that gold refining was certainly mastered by New Kingdom times, if not earlier.

A deliberate alloying with other metals, particularly copper, iron and sometimes platinum, gives much of the ancient gold work a grey, reddish-brown or plum-purple patina because of the secondary components (XIV).

Silver was also found in solid beads in Nakada II sites. However, not untll New Kingdom times was it worked in equal quality and quantity to gold. Called "white gold," Egyptian silver of the Old and Middle Kingdoms had a gold content composition from 9% to as high as 38%. Being rarer in Egypt than gold, silver was more highly valued than the former until the Middle Kingdom when it began to be imported from Asiatic sources. Aside from the objects plundered, much of the ancient silver corroded due to contact with salt-impregnated soil (unlike gold).

Mainly gold and electrum, but also some silver, were used, aside from these metals being made into objects per se, for setting of gemstones.

The high standard of craftsmanship in fashioning the "noble metals" was based more on the quality of the materials used, the time spent on each piece and, above all, the skill of the jewellers, rather than the crude tools available to them. The methods adopted were those commonly used throughout the Near East. Repousse, chasing, and, from Middle Kingdom times onwards, granulation work was applied. Typical of Egyptian jewellery is the open-work pectoral. Cloisonne inlays of semi-precious stones or glass were usually held in position by a bed of cement. A method related to cloisonne, albeit used more in the Aegean area, was niello (in it an alloy of copper, sulphur and lead is pressed into the cells); it is evidenced in only a few examples from ancient Egypt. Engraving was done only after iron had come into general use, and tools of this metal were available. The cire-perdue method of hollow casting was also applied (in a similar way, false teeth are made now). Statuettes and other small articles were cast solid.

Wooden furniture would be covered with a thick sheet of gold, hammered onto it directly and fixed with small gold rivets. Or, on a prepared base of plaster or glue, thinner gold sheets might be attached, and the finest of gold leaf would be used to cover statues, mummy masks, coffins and other funerary equipment.

GEMSTONES

The Egyptians used two different words for stones, one for the "noble materials" or precious and semi-precious stones (others = "beautiful stones"). These were not, in jewellery-making, chosen for their sparkle, but rather their rich colours.

The classic trio comprised the red carnelian, blue and green turquoise and lapis lazuli. All three were known to be used from predynastic times. Green felspar, the Amazon stone, was sometimes used as a substitute for turquoise, as it is occassionally distinctly blue, although generally, of an opaque rich green tint. Carnelian, easily picked up in pebbles, came from The Eastern Desert, while turquoise was mined from veins in the sandstone of Sinai, the "Green Land." Lapis lazuli (Egyptian: Khebshbed) imported via the Euphrates trading route from Badakshan/Afghanistan, was because of its foreign origin, very expensive. The artificial replacement for lapis lazuli, in use since Dynasty IV or before, owed its deep blue colour to a copper calcium tetrasilicate used in the production.

The mes-at or "purveyor of precious stones" mentioned in a papyrus, was probably one of the prospectors roving the desert for stones to be made into amulets, inlays into wood or gold settings, or beads and scarabs.

Other semi-precious stones were much in use, such as amethysts, occurring in granite-rock cavities of the Aswan and Eastern Desert districts, (worked into one of King Djoser's, Dynasty III, bracelets). The height of its popularity was during Middle Kingdom times.

Garnets of a very small variety came from Aswan, while larger specimens were found in Western Sinai, making this stone also a particularly favoured one in the Middle Kingdom, due to intensive mining activity in the area at the time.

Green and brown jaspers, rock-crystal, obsidian, banded chalcedony and agate were worked only sporadically in Pharaonic times.

Beryl was not used until the Hellenistic Period. In Tutankh-amun's time, a transparent type of calcite, Iceland spar and rock-crystal were used as inlay atop a coloured cement backing. These and other natural and artificial substitutes for classical gemstones were introduced. The Egyptian description for glass was "melted stone." It is often difficult to tell the man-made article from that "provided by the gods."

Hathor, the chief deity of the desert, was particularly associated with jewellery; she was also the patron of miners and prospectors (XXIX). The cult object her priestesses are shown wearing or carrying was an elaborate multi-stranded bead necklace with a metal counterpoise called Menyet (29 & 41).

29) MENYET

This cult object of Hathor consists of strands of blue faience ring beads, connected to the necklace proper of much heavier beads by caps of a bronze cone on either end. The necklace in turn is fitted with a counterpoise of bronze (also: 41).

The menyet was carried by queens and great ladies acting as, or by priestesses of, Hathor, as symbol of their devotion to this goddess' cult. On rare occasions, the menyet was worn by priests of Hathor; King Amen-em-het of Dyn. XII is shown with one. Also the moon-god Khons is sometimes represented with a menyet.

Usually, ladies carrying this object are holding a sistrum with a Hathor-head as well, distinguishing them as "Singer of Amun," since Hathor is also the goddess of dance and music.

This specimen is an actual object for use by the living and, as such, rare.

NECKLACES

Jewellery, worn by both sexes, is not only one of the most pleasing, but also the most abundantly found type of antiquity from Egypt.

Necklaces practically formed part of daily custom, at least for the class of people whose circumstances permitted this. The re-stringing of necklaces is of necessity arbitrary, as only very rarely multi-component necklaces were found intact. However, the re-assembling of jewellery is greatly aided by many detailed descriptions from tomb paintings, so that a fair degree of accuracy can be achieved in this respect.

The Baba (faience-maker or firer of glaze) was a specialist, as was the skilled necklace-worker (Setro). The maker of beads was called Iru-Weshbet and, as other artists and craftsmen, was engaged in one production only. Ancient Egypt's bead-industry is the single most important contribution to jewellery-making. It remained unequalled by any other people in variety of shape, substance and the use they were put to.

As early as Neolithic times, Egyptian beads were made of pebbles, seeds, shells, horn, bones and, somewhat later, glazed steatite and then faience.

Pebble-drilling for beads was usually done from opposite poles to prevent the hole from "wandering," usually with the bow-drill. Often three drill-stocks were operated with one bow, as seen in many tomb paintings. As accurate drilling by this method is not likely, perhaps it represents polishing.

Pebbles of carnelian, jasper, crystal, agate, amethyst and garnet were widely used for elegant necklaces. Faience remained throughout a favoured component of necklaces. Small amulets were often interspersed into strings of beads, and gold might enhance the value of such pieces (XXIXa). The size of beads varied enormously. The high point of achievement of the bead-maker was reached during the Middle Kingdom; from that time come beads of minute size and extraordinary fineness.

FAIENCE, GLAZED STONES, GLASS

Faience and glazed compositions are the materials more typically used for plastic arts of the dynastic period of Egypt than terracotta. Faience is an Egyptian invention, evidently developed by a people living on the Libyan border, hence the name (Fayum). From predynastic times, it had appeared mostly in the form of beads, either with the core of faience or of solid quartz or steatite. Glazed beads were made also from Badarian times on, as well as small amulets and pendants. The precise method of glazing is unknown. Presumably the mass was applied to the core as a viscous fluid coating the object, then both were fused by heat, thus giving the finished product its coherence and strength.

41) MENKHET (COUNTER-POISE) OF QUEEN TIYE — BRONZE

Such counterpoises formed part of the menyet, the cult object carried by priestesses of Hathor, and all other types of wide and relatively heavy, necklaces requiring a counter-weight on the back of the wearer. Some of the extant menkhets of funerary use were made of plain sheet-gold or cloisonne-work. Counterpoises up to the New Kingdom consisted of two pieces of bronze, thereafter of only one.

This bronze open-work type has three representations of Hathor: at top, in the likeness of the queen, the head surmounted by the lyriform horns alongside the solar disk, on a uraeus modius, with a Broad Collar necklace completing the image. Within the vertical parts Tiye-Hathor, holding a papyrus sceptre, stands. Below, the goddess in her disguise as the cow with the solar disk, standing on a papyrus skiff and emerging from the papyrus thicket of the western mountains, in her function as protector of the dead.

Bronze open-work objects from the time of Amenophix III, husband of Tiye, are not uncommon.

The faience composition consisted of a core of small quartz grains or rock crystal which had been ground into a fine powder. This was light and friable but without coherence. While the binding method used is not clear, it was possibly achieved by a weak sodium carbonate solution which was chemically combined by heat with the powder. In this state, the mass could be worked with fingers, cast, carved, shaped and fired. Since small objects in this material could be produced cheaply, the composition was used extensively for beads, pendants, rings, funerary equipment (such as amulets and pectorals), or tiles for house decorations, particularly in houses and palaces from the Amarna Period and Ramesside times (XXXIV).

The colours most commonly used for faience and glazing were blue, green or greenish-blue, the latter achieved by the addition of a copper compound. A particularly vivid blue is characteristic of New Kingdom objects, and a combination of dark blue on light blue typical of Dynasty XXX.

White, yellow and red became frequently used colours for faience and glazing from the middle of Dynasty XVIII onwards. Polychrome faience work reached its highest stage of development during the Amarna Period.

These small objects for daily use and as part of funerary equipment are a testimony of the taste and artistic genius of the ancient Egyptians and are more important in this respect than any other class of antiquities. Throughout her history, Egypt remained preeminent in this craft.

The natural fauna and flora of the Nile Valley were the main inspirations for decoration of work in faience and glazed stones.

Glazing of pottery by means of lead glazes was done only from Roman times on.

Glass was not independently used as a medium until Dynasty XVIII, except for some sporadic production of small beads and amulets. The technique was a natural development of that of glazing. However, the core for glass vessels was of sandy clay which, on completion of the manufacture, was removed. It is possible that the introduction of this new type of vessel was due to contacts with Syria following the military conquests during Dynasty XVIII. This theory is based on the long interval between production of faience objects and that of glass vessels. The latter were made in coloured, sometimes polychromed glass, but were not transparent. Most objects of glass were no more than 5" high, and were usually pots for eye-paint or perfume jars with lids, or other cosmetic containers. Glass was also utilised for the inlay of profile faces of royal persons. Figurines in this medium are rare. Glass was never used as extensively as faience. In the Late Period it does not seem to have been made at all, but reappeared in Ptolemaic times. With the invention of glass blowing during the first century B. C., glass was in common use and Egypt, together with Syria, during the Roman Period, was one of the main centres of its production (XXXV).

SPICES AND COSMETICS

The use of scents and ointments in the primitive hygenic conditions of ancient days was as much a necessity as a luxury. Perfumes and spices were used as ingredients for perfumed oils, ointments and powder. The essence of flowers was extracted by pressing. Many tomb paintings and reliefs show this method of wringing the fragrant substances in cloths to squeeze out the odoriferous liquids (42). Seeds and fruits of acacia and teak, etc. were soaked in oil or water to produce perfumes. Resins were a basic ingredient in cosmetics, used either in powder form or dissolved in oils and mixed with other substances in the production of ointments. Cosmetic oils had as their base animal fats or cedar oil. Pigments for tinting the hair, face, finger-and toenails were extensively used, including in the mummification process. An important ingredient for lip rouge, found in a cosmetic jar from approx. 2500 B. C. was red antimony ore, a poisonous metal with cherry red crystals. It is a brittle metallic substance with flaky crystalline texture. Gray antimony, the more common species, was used as the basis of many Egyptian ointments. Lip rouge was applied with the tip of a brush. Archeologists have found quantities of utensils for the manufacture of, as well as for crushing, mixing, storing and applying cosmetics. The latter was done either with the finger, tiny spatulae or spoons of wood, bone and from the Roman Period, mainly bronze.

42) RECTANGULAR LIMESTONE SLAB — BAS RELIEF SHOWING CRUSHING LILIES — PTOLEMAIC

Lirinon, the perfumed unguent generally used by a number of ancient peoples, consisted mainly of the essence of lilies.

The figures here show a degree of foreshortening, which had been mastered in relief carving by Ptolemaic times, as well as some motion. A peculiarity of the period are pointed breasts and short hair fitting the head like a cap.

Part of a larger scene of the work of extracting essence, this illustrates two women twisting with long sticks a net full of lilies above a high-necked jar with a wide brim into which the liquid flows. Quite realistically, the stick on the left is bending slightly under the pressure of the motion.

43) CAST BRONZE SITULA PTOLEMAIC PERIOD

The vessel was used in the libation of life-giving water (and other liquids) in funerary rites. The hemispherical base bears an embossed design of lotus petals and leaves. The relief scenes of the main register include the deceased in front of an offering table, the ithyphallic god Min and a number of other deities, seven in all. Tablets above the gods and goddesses relate their names and ranks. Strangely, the tablet above the head of the deceased was left uninscribed, thus preventing identification of ownership of the situla.

The illustrated side shows the falcon-headed Horus, "Son of Osiris," wearing the Pshent = Double Crown, and Isis, followed by Nephthys. All three carry the WAS sceptre for power and the ankh sign. Below the inscribed top register are reliefs of the mythical boats of day and night sailing from left to right. The visible end-portion of the boat of night is drawn by four jackals. It was believed to be the boat used by the sun-god during the twelve hours of night on his journey along the River of Hell.

The prestige associated with cosmetics is evidenced by their often precious and beautifully worked containers (XVI), such as the fifty unguent vases found in Tut-ankh-amun's tomb. Heavy and perhaps difficult to move, they were emptied of their valuable contents on the second visit of the grave robbers while other, seemingly more precious objects were left untouched. In religious texts reference is made to particular goddesses whose perfume was stronger than that of others, showing the importance of cosmetics in the minds of the ancient Egyptians. Ointments, powders and perfumes played a very important role in rituals (43). Products for this purpose were manufactured in small temple-laboratories. One of these is still intact at Edfu; the walls of the room are covered with prescriptions, after quite complicated formulae, for the various concoctions. The ritual of offering incense to the gods is frequently shown in carvings, tomb paintings, etc. It served the dual purpose of fulfilling a religious duty as well as temporarily purifying the air. Censers and incense bowls were used for this, as well as puffing it through incense ladles. Both men and women used cosmetics. Scenes depicting festivals and banquets show a method of applying perfume by placing a scented grease cone atop a person's head. This cone was recapped by servant girls whenever the dripping fat had melted down too far (XXX). Through international trade cosmetics and spices reached Egypt, some from the Far East. It is not yet clear how they found their way from those distant lands. Beginning in Dynasty V expeditions were sent periodically to Punt, somewhere on the coast of Somaliland, and the South Arabian kingdoms to obtain "incense trees" and a great number of basics needed for the industry. Some of the ingredients for cosmetics and spices were:

ALOE

A perfume from the resin of a special tree grown in North India and Malay, still in use for cult purposes in some parts of Asia. The juice of it is bitter; a purgative drug is still being made from it.

BALSAM

Extracted from the resin of the Opobalsamum tree, growing in the region of Mecca. Its excellence of fragrance, as well as its high price are mentioned in many records.

CASSIA

There are two types but only the cassia of China, produced from the aromatic inner bark of the tree was used. It figures in records as one of the most costly items of the industry. It was one of the ingredients for cosmetic oil, as well as incense. Cincamon-cassia was used as a spice.

FRANKINCENSE

Aromatic gum resin from a tree growing in India, Somaliland, southern parts of Arabia; it was the most important of all incense, used throughout the Near East. This ingredient was known in all Semitic languages by the same term.

GALBANUM

"Green incense," a gum resin from a particular species of a Persian ferula.

HENNA

A domestic privet, a bushy evergreen shrub with fragrant flowers growing in clusters. Its shoots and leaves were ground and dissolved in water to produce the yellowish pigment used for dying hair, teeth and nails. Mummies were also painted with henna. As a medicine, it was used in cases of urinary disease.

LADANUM (LAUDANUM, LADANON)

A gummy substance extracted from the leaves of the citrus plant throughout the Mediterranean but not, as yet, in pharaonic Egypt. It is still collected by shepherds with a flail-like implement called ladanisterion.

MYRRH

One of the most important perfumes of kings, it was also used for incense-making and in medicine. Myrrh is extracted by means of incision of the bark from a sweet, aromatic cicely plant growing in South Arabia and Punt. It was a precious gift and much used by women.

NARD

An aromatic plant, its perfume mainly used by women, it grew in Nepal and the Himalayas, imported via India and Persia. Its Sanskrit name NADALA means odoriferous. The essence was extracted by two different means which decided the price of the end-product: either by soaking the leaves in oil, or gathering it from the spikes.

46) ALABASTRON

Alabaster — beautiful wave-pattern — with flat, wide lip and simulated lug handles without holes — interior wall shows flecks of darkish cosmetic matter. The name of the vessel is derived from the most frequently used medium in its manufacture (C. 606)

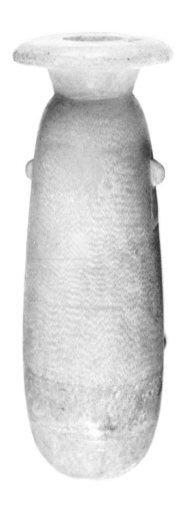

Containers for cosmetics and spices were made in an infinite variety of shapes, as well as materials. Occasional New Kingdom examples have even been found of cosmetic vessels being carried by or atop representations of human figures (15). Containers were fitted with a lid or a contraption or reed strips to keep the ointments fresh. Some of the tiny containers, the manufacture of which began with the general expansion of the stone vase industry during the Nakada II Period of prehistoric Egypt, may have contained malachite paste (XV). Cylindrical- or barrel-shaped miniature pots must have been part of elegant toilet outfits. Presumably difficult to produce because of the hardness of the stones and their small size, they had a special charm.

In the later period little kohl pots were made of faience; one made for royalty bears the cartouches of the respective king and his consort. Some double kohl vases are extant. Kohl tubes were also made of ivory with relief carving or in the shape of human figures. Kohl and containers for it were commonly found in Badarian graves. For its manufacture, the lead sulphide, galena, obtained from the region of Elephantine (Aswan), the Red Sea Coast, Punt or the Near East, was used, mixed with goose fat. The kohl was applied inside the wide, green band of malachite paste on the eyelids. Eyebrows were blackened with it as well. A heightened effect was obtained by using a double line of kohl to elongate the line of the eyes from both levels outwards to beyond the cheekbones. Both sexes practised this cosmetic custom (44-46).

Cosmetic implements of limestone were made also in the shape of small dishes for mixing cosmetics; they were wide-rimmed and shallow and were used as the descendents of the cosmetic palettes of schist etc. in use during the Prehistoric and into the Dynastic Period of Egypt.

Cosmetic spoons were made of ivory and bone and, infrequently, of silver and slate (XXXI). In a grave from Badarian times, tiny cosmetic spoons were found together with horns to hold cosmetic powder. The little spoons were used through a slot near the tip of the horn which was then closed with a stopper, another stopper closing the refill base of the horn. It has been pointed out that the modern Ba-Suto tribe of West Africa uses such horns and small spoons for their snuff and that there is a strong possibility of similar contents in the horns of the ancient Egyptians. Another function of this horn and spoon implement could be as salt storer or dispenser. Some stoppers on unguent bottles were shaped as spoons. By inverting the bottle, the liquid could be drawn off into the spoon through an opening at the lower end of the bowl of the spoon.

44) SCENE FROM LIMESTONE SARCOPHAGUS OF QUEEN KAWIT, DYN. XI.

During the earlier part of the Middle Kingdom, a highly refined but not flamboyant style marks much of the relief work. The somewhat stiff, elongated figures are characteristic of the first years of the reign of Mentu-hotep II, husband of Kawit. Careful drawing and a most exacting technique in this very slight sunk relief are distinctive of the short-lived style.

The outer sides of sarcophagi of royal ladies from the early Middle Kingdom who were buried at Deir el-Bahri were decorated with scenes from daily life; on the other side of this one is a scene showing the milking of a cow, and others.

The type of chair is known from Dynasty II representations, but this example has a lower stretcher than the earlier kind. High-backed, with rectangular open arm-rests, it has a cushion thrown over the back.

Kawit drinks milk from a shallow cup, holding in the other hand a flat metal disk mirror (4). A female attendant dresses her coiffure of a multitude of tiny plaits.

This is but one of the innumerable hairstyles favoured by both sexes, with a great variety for each of them. Ointments for scalp treatment, against baldness, grey hair, fixatives, and others, were in frequent use.

The artist has achieved the greatest degree of naturalism in the rendering of the "hairdresser."

45) OINTMENT JAR AND LID

Alabaster — barrel-shape with wide flat lip and narrow opening to fit protrusion inside flat lid — probably to store malachite (C. 609)

48) SPINDLE WHORL
of ivory, with flat, undecorated underside and annuloid design for the top. C. 884

BOBBIN OR POSSIBLY BEAD
of ivory, with striation design for the top and flat, undecorated underside. The similarity between spindle whorls and large beads often makes a clear distinction impossible. C. 887

IVORY SPINDLES
one with ring top. C. 888
    Spindle whorls of the Middle Kingdom were generally flat and cylindrical, while those from the New Kingdom were dome-shaped. The shaft of the spindle remained unchanged throughout. The distaff came into use only in Roman times. Spinning was done by women until the New Kingdom; afterwards by both sexes. One or two spindle weights were placed at the end of the rod.

SPINNING AND WEAVING

    Spindle whorls were found in Badarian village sites from the Early Prehistoric Period. However, some doubt exists as to the exact function of the pierced pottery disks, but any use other than for spinning for them seems hard to imagine, even though many of them are somewhat lightweight for the purpose (48).

    They are rarely found in graves, as is true of all tools of the Prehistoric Period. They were made of wood, stone or pottery, or of ivory and bone. Most of our knowledge relating to spinning and weaving in the whole of the Near East is derived from the many specimens of cloth, usually linen, which have survived because of the dry climate of Egypt, as well as the numerous tomb paintings or clay models pertaining to the craft.

    Flax was cultivated from Neolithic times onwards. Pictorial representations show its cultivation, as well as the various stages of turning the fibres into yarn and the yarn into cloth. Flax was not cut like crops but pulled up by the roots. Because of the strength of hand needed to do this, flax-gathering is referred to in descriptions of the king seizing his enemies, and tying them into "bundles" by the hair, alluding to the superhuman strength of the ruler.

    Weaving was done at the upper part of the loom, the woven cloth rolled on top of the beam, inserted through the warp with the fingers at the beginning. Later thin rods of ivory or bone or wood were employed for the purpose.

    Until the Middle Kingdom there was no wool-producing breed of sheep in Egypt. A possible religious taboo against the use of woollen garments throughout the Dynastic Period may also account for the scarcity of extant specimens of wool. Linen was used for clothing, shrouds and mummy wrappings, sails for boats, medical dressings, etc. It was produced from the coarsest heavy cloth to the finest cambric to which the Old Testament frequently refers as Byssus (Greek). The high skill of the weaver of Egypt throughout her history was well known.

    During the New Kingdom, tapestry-weaving and needlepoint embroidery was used for the luxurious fashions of the day. The few examples from Tut-ankh-amun's tomb which have survived show this court version of the ancient craft. Silk was used from Ptolemaic times onwards only. However, as an import article, cotton, "wool from a tree" had figured in the annals of a pharaoh from the sixth century B. C. Cotton generally was used, in Egypt itself, from Coptic times on.

Dress was regularly white until the New Kingdom, worn draped and pleated, not tailored, while the few extant representations of coloured dress are usually worn by foreigners. Most examples of textiles date from Coptic times and bear little resemblance to pharaonic style and decoration. Burial equipment during dynastic times usually included lengths of cloth, intended for the daily use of the deceased, complete with hieratic inscriptions as to the name of the owner, the quality of the cloth and date of its use.

Horizontal looms were used for the weaving of mats made of coarse grass, rush or reed. Early dynastic architecture reproduced patterns of mat weaves, and was to remain one of the dominant artistic motifs of the period. The earliest of these are the blue glass-composition tile decorations imitating mat hangings in mastaba rooms of the Step Pyramid of King Djoser of Dynasty III. One fragment of woven reed matting from Badarian times exists. One small piece of woven linen, from between 3800–3300 B. C., showing advanced skill, is a 2-ply thread with 20–25 warp threads and 25–30 weft threads per square inch (XXXVI).

49) SCHIST LOOM WEIGHT of dome shape, with a flat underside of circular grooving. C. 844.

WEIGHING

The most ancient of all standards and measures are those of Egypt (and Babylon) with the decimal system of the Egyptians in use outside the country as well. Numerous scenes of metal weighing from tomb paintings as well as those depicting the "Weighing of the Heart" show the Egyptian balance in its basic principle of a wooden beam suspended from the centrepoint by a cord, with metal pans, unaltered, if modified, throughout the Dynastic Period. Alterations to ensure greater accuracy in the balance were made as time went on. Often the beam was surmounted by a representation of Ma'at, the goddess of truth with the emblematic feather atop her head.

Merchants carried the weights on their persons. Authority-approved weights were called the "king's weights."

Weights for the gold standard and usually inscribed with its hieroglyphic sign "Nub" are the most common of standards. The weight of metal in texts from the New Kingdom is generally given in a number of DEBEN, divided into ten KITE, i. e. about 91 grammes (or 140 grains). Different values of the same basic units were used for different commodities, a method still practised in some places.

Weights were sometimes made in the shape of a human head; one particularly fine example dates from the 14th century B. C.

GLOSSARY

AKHENATEN (Amenophis IV) king from 1379–1362 B.C., the "heretic" who introduced the sun-disk, Aten, as the monotheistic faith, abolishing the multitude of previously worshipped god-cults. He dictated a style in art of stark realism, known after his newly erected capital city, Amarna.

AMARNA STYLE based on the king's unusual physical characteristics, it created a type of portraiture, verging often on the grotesque, but with a great deal of realism. Along with the Aten-disk of Akhenaten's monotheism, this veristic style was already evident in the reign of that king's father and the king ruling immediately before him.

AMARNA, TELL el correctly: Et-Till, el-Amarna; the site in Middle Egypt where, in about 1370 B.C., the new capital of the king of Egypt was built, after he had removed the court from Thebes. Its name translates into "Horizon-of-the-Aten" (Aton). Situated on the west bank of the Nile, it is now a Bedouin encampment.

AMEN-EM-HET (Amen-emes) the name of four kings of the Middle Kingdom's strong Dynasty XII.

AMENOPHIS four outstanding monarchs of the New Kingdom bore this name.

BA the soul of the deceased, represented as a bird with a human head. Unlike the KA, who was to be left stationary, the BA was free to visit the world of the living and return to the tomb.

BOOK OF THE DEAD written in hieroglyphic, hieratic or demotic script, these were excerpts from religious funerary texts, on papyrus or leather and placed into the tombs of important people. Consisting of drawings and incantations, they were to ensure by their very existence, or by being read out loud, a happy after-life. Many different compositions of its kind were used, but all bore the title, in accordance with the intended purpose, "Formula for going forth by day."

CANOPIC JARS receptacles, mainly of alabaster, holding the embalmed viscera after mummification.

CARTOUCHE originating from a double rope-loop with a knot at its base (sign for "eternity" = "that which encircles the sun"), it developed into the elongated shape to accomodate the king's name, expressing the idea that the world belonged to Pharaoh.

CROWNS worn by ancient Egyptian kings and gods. The symbolic significance of some of the multitude of different shaped crowns has not been established.

DELTA area at the mouth of the Nile, of fertile alluvial soil.

ENNEAD (Egyptian: Pesedjet) group of nine deities, representing the elemental forces in the universe.

FAYUM a deep oasis-depression in the Libyan Desert, to the west of Middle Egypt, Connected to the Nile by a natural branch of the river, called in Coptic "River of Joseph."

HELIOPOLIS north-east of Cairo in the desert, it has one of the (four or five) remaining obelisks still standing in Egypt (that of Sesostris I of Dynasty XII). From earliest dynastic times, the sun was worshipped there under a variety of names, aided by the cult-fetish Ben-Ben, (forerunner of the obelisk) on which the sun was thought to rise.

KA the intangible being, the "spirit" on ancient Egyptian belief, for whose contentment in the after-life of the dead elaborate provisions were made. In hieroglyphics, it is represented as two raised arms connected by a horizontal ground line.

LIBYANS nomadic inhabitants of the region west of the Delta, herdsmen and tree-planters whose physical characteristics and customs resembled those of some of the groups of Egypt. Both wore what is often called KAMATA, a belt with an oblong penis sheath. Blue-eyed and with blond hair unlike other African ethnic groups, they began to harrass Egypt in great numbers in about 1400 B.C. Ultimately, by means of settling as mercenaries for centuries, they gained the throne of Egypt as the Libyan or Bubastite Dynasty, 935–730 B.C.

MANETHO trained in a sacerdotal college, this priest-historian living in the early third century B.C. wrote among other works the Aegyptiaca ("History of Egypt"), preserved in parts only. Mainly his work included lists of royal names in chronological order, but because of later abbreviations, the veracity of lengths of reigns etc. is often in doubt.

MEMPHIS (Greek; Egyptian: Men-nofer) first capital city of the kings of dynastic Egypt, situated 17 miles south of Cairo.

NEW KINGDOM third and last period of Egypt's greatness — begun after the expulsion of the Hyksos rulers of Dynasty XVI, (invading settlers of Asiatic stock in the Delta region) by Theban princes of Dynasty XVII, it commences as Dynasty XVIII in about 1567 B.C. Expansive foreign policy, economic revival, somewhat ostentatious display of luxury in art characterise the age. One of the early kings of the New Kingdom instituted the custom of building his tomb into the rock in the Valley of the Kings at Thebes, in contrast to the hitherto used pyramid burials, much more vulnerable to grave robbings.

NOMARCH term derived from the Greek word NOME for administrative districts of dynastic Egypt and denoting the governing official of the respective provinces.

OGDOAD group of eight deities; four couples who, as the elemental forces preceded the creation of the world, in accordance with legends from Hermopolis.

OSIRID PILLAR architectural member on the outside of temples, in the shape of the mummified god Osiris, king of the dead.

PTOLEMAIC the period called after the fifteen kings named Ptolemy who ruled Egypt after the death of Alexander the Great until the suicide of Cleopatra Philopater VII in 30 B.C.

RAMESSIDES eleven kings called Ramesses, on the throne of Egypt from 1320 B.C. until the end of the New Kingdom in 1085 B.C., of Dynasty XIX and XX. The first of the name completed the liquidation of the religious regime of monotheism, brought on by Akhenaten. The two most outstanding kings were Ramesses II and, as the last great king of the New Kingdom, Ramesses III.

SAITE the Dynasty of native princes from Sais in the Delta, ruling Egypt as the XXVIth Dynasty, bringing about a renaissance of sculpture, based largely on close studies of antiquities.

SCARAB the sacred beetle of Egyptian religious belief (scarabeus sacer). Its shape was the model for innumerable seals, amulets and part of the funerary equipment in a great variety of materials.

SERDAB Arabic for "cellar" = a small chamber within the tomb to house a statue of the deceased.

SESOSTRIS the name of three kings of the Middle Kingdom of whom Sesostris III, later deified, brought Dynasty XII to the height of its power. He abolished the authority of the nomarchs, whose ascent to enormous political influence had played a disastrous part in the collapse of the Old Kingdom.

STELA an upright slab of stone with carved and painted inscriptions pertaining to funerary rites. Its function was as a tomb stone, but also as boundary marker.

TUTHMOSIS the name of four kings from the New Kingdom. The most famous was Tuthmosis III, "Hero of the Age," nominally king during the reign of Queen Hatshepsut but in fact, after her rule.

URAEUS cobra-goddess of Lower Egypt. As the personal god of the kings, it is shown on the brow-part of royal headdresses, on cornices of royal shrines, etc.

USHABTI older name: shawabti, a word possibly derived from the persea or shabab tree, which provided the raw material for these. The precise origin of the older term was lost as long ago as ancient Egyptian times. Ushabti = "answerer" in Arabic. It denotes the small mummiform human figurines of wood, faience etc., inscribed with magical spells and particularly texts in which the ushabti, as the stand-in for the deceased is ordered to comply with the call-up for the corvee duties in the hereafter.

VALLEY OF THE KINGS in the western mountain lies the heart of the Theban necropolis, where the kings of the New Kingdom, beginning with Tuthmosis I, had their rock-hewn tombs cut into the cliffs, in favour of previously used pyramids.

VALLEY OF THE QUEENS a modest variety of the Valley of the Kings, this burial place called "The Place of Beauty" (Arabic: Biban el-Harim) is located at the southern end of the Theban necropolis, In it are buried the "Wives" and "Daughters of the King" of the Ramesside era.

REFERENCE ACKNOWLEDGMENTS

Cyril Aldred: Akhenaten and Nefer-titi, Viking Press, 1973

Cyril Aldred: Jewels of the Pharaohs, Praeger Publ., New York, 1971

Cyril Aldred: At henaten, Pharaoh of Egypt, a new study, Sphere Books Ltd., London, 1972

Cyril Aldred: The Egyptians, Thames & Hudson, London, 1961

Cyril Aldred: Development of ancient Egyptian art, Academy Editions, London, 1973

Art of World series (I. Woldering): The art of the Egyptians, 1963

Art of World series (du Bouguet): The art of the Copts, 1971

Elise Baumgartel: The cultures of prehistoric Egypt (II), Oxford University Press, 1960

The Brooklyn Museum of Fine Arts: Five years of collecting Egyptian art, John B. Watkins Co., 1956

Boston Museum of Fine Arts: Ancient Egypt, N.Y. Graphic Society, 1960

Boston Fine Arts Museum: Treasures of Egyptian art from the Cairo Museum, Thames & Hudson, London, 1970

Trustees of the British Museum: Introductory Guide to the Egyptian Collection, 1969

Trustees of the British Museum: Treasures of Tut-ankh-amun, 1972

Christiane Desroches-Noblecourt: Tut-ankh-amun, Penguin, 1971

Egyptian State Tourist Administration, Cairo: Egyptian Museum, Cairo, 1959

Warwick and Trump: The Penguin Dictionary of Archaeology, 1970

Georges Posener: Dictionary of Egyptian civilisation, Tudor Publ., New York, 1959

Hannelore Kischkewitz: Egyptian drawings, Octopus Books, 1972

New Larousse Encyclopedia of Mythology, Hamlyn Publ., 1968

Boris de Rachewitz: An introduction to Egyptian art, Hutchinson & Co., England, 1966

Alan Rowe: Catalogue of Egyptian scarabs, L'Institute Francais d'archaeologie Orientale, 1936

Ernesto Scammezi: Egyptian art in the Egyptian Museum of Turin, Harry N. Abrams, 1965

Monochrome—

1   Predynastic cosmetic palettes, C. 620, 619
1a Arrowheads
2   Butt for dagger
3   Adzehead
4   Mirror
5   Reserve head
6   Seated scribe
7   Statue of Si-Kahiha
8   Dancing dwarfs
9   Head of Sesostris III
10 Sphinx of Amen-em-het III
11 Ebony figure of court official
12 Limestone statue of Nefer-titi
13 Granite statue of Tuthmosis III
14 The god Ptah
15 Small wooden figure of girl with unguent jar
16 Clasped hands
17 Sketch of the head of Akhenaten
18 Ebony small-scale statue of a court lady
19 Sunk relief of herdsman and goat
20 Akhenaten and one of his daughters
21 Sunk relief of Akhenaten as sphinx
22 Domestic cult statue
23 Granite statue of Ramesses II
24 Sunk relief of the head of Sethos I
25 Granite bust of a Ptolemaic queen
26 Porphyry bust of a Caesar
27 Coptic relief & fresco painting
28 List of major gods
29 Hathor cult-object: menyet
30 Amulets
31 Ivory panel with Thoeris and Bes figures
32 Limestone Janus-head of Hathor
33 Cylinder seal—Archaic Period
34 Silver alloy seal and scarab
35 3 scarabs
36 3 scarabs
37 3 scarabs
38 Faience ushabti
39 Rhind mathematical papyrus
40 Canons of human proportions
41 Counterpoise for the menyet
42 Bas relief on limestone slab: crushing lilies
43 Cast bronze situla
44 Relief on limestone sarcophagus
45 Alabaster cosmetic jar with lid
46 Alabastron
47 Clay oil lamp
48 Implements for spinning
49 Loom weight
50 Coptic textiles

Note: Objects, for which the captions are marked with the letter C., are from the Herbert E. Clark Collection, Jerusalem.

Colour plates—

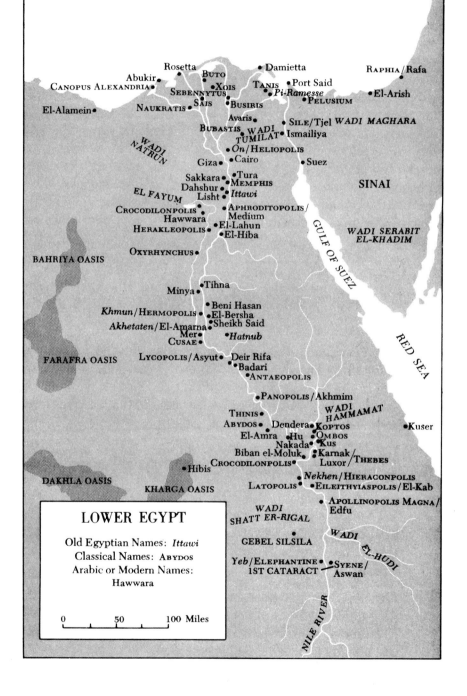

MEDITERRANEAN SEA

Rosetta • • Damietta

RAPHIA/Rafa

Abukir • BUTO Port Said

CANOPUS ALEXANDRIA • XOIS TANIS Pi-Ramesse

SEBENNYTUS El-Arish

El-Alamein • NAUKRATIS SAIS BUSIRIS PELUSIUM

Avaris SILE/Tjel WADI MAGHARA

BUBASTIS WADI Ismailiya
TUMILAT

WADI On/HELIOPOLIS
NATRUN

Giza • Cairo • Suez

Sakkara • Tura SINAI

Dahshur MEMPHIS

EL FAYUM Lisht • Ittawi WADI SERABIT
EL-KHADIM

CROCODILONPOLIS • APHRODITOPOLIS/
Hawwara Medium

HERAKLEOPOLIS • El-Lahun
El-Hiba

OXYRHYNCHUS •

BAHRIYA OASIS

GULF OF SUEZ

Minya • Tihna

Beni Hasan
KHMUN/HERMOPOLIS • El-Bersha
Sheikh Said

Akhetaten/El-Amarna RED SEA
Mer
CUSAE • Hatnub

FARAFRA OASIS

LYCOPOLIS/Asyut • Deir Rifa
Badari
ANTAEOPOLIS

PANOPOLIS/Akhmim

WADI
HAMMAMAT

THINIS

ABYDOS Dendera KOPTOS Kuser
El-Amra Hu OMBOS
Nakada Kus
Biban el-Moluk Karnak
CROCODILONPOLIS Luxor THEBES

Hibis NEKHEN/HIERACONPOLIS

DAKHLA OASIS Latopolis EILEITHYIASPOLIS/El-Kab

KHARGA OASIS APOLLINOPOLIS MAGNA/
Edfu

WADI
SHATT ER-RIGAL WADI
EL-HUDI

LOWER EGYPT GEBEL SILSILA

Old Egyptian Names: *Ittawi* Yeb/ELEPHANTINE SYENE/
1ST CATARACT Aswan

Classical Names: ABYDOS

Arabic or Modern Names:
Hawwara NILE RIVER

0   50   100 Miles

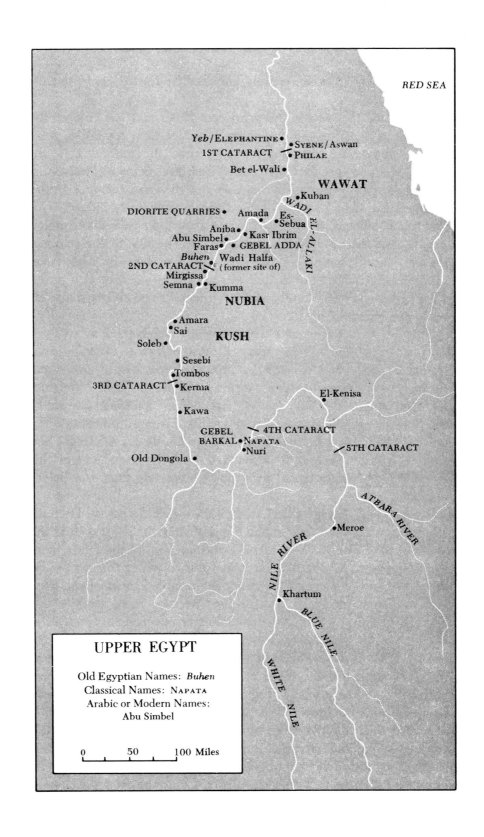

RED SEA

Yeb/ELEPHANTINE •
• SYENE / Aswan
1ST CATARACT
• PHILAE

Bet el-Wali •

WAWAT

• Kuban

DIORITE QUARRIES •   Amada •
• Es-
Sebua

Aniba •   ZZ
Abu Simbel •   • Kasr Ibrim
Faras •   • GEBEL ADDA

Buhen   Wadi Halfa
2ND CATARACT   (former site of)
Mirgissa •
Semna •   • Kumma

NUBIA

• Amara
• Sai

Soleb •   **KUSH**

• Sesebi
• Tombos
3RD CATARACT   • Kerma

• Kawa

• El-Kenisa

GEBEL   4TH CATARACT
BARKAL • Napata
• Nuri   5TH CATARACT
Old Dongola •

WADI EL-ALLAKI

ATBARA RIVER

NILE RIVER   • Meroe

• Khartum

BLUE NILE

WHITE NILE

UPPER EGYPT

Old Egyptian Names: *Buhen*
Classical Names: NAPATA
Arabic or Modern Names:
Abu Simbel

0   50   100 Miles

95

96